STRENGTH

for the

MOMENT

Given to: ....

From: ....

Date: ....

Special Message:

STRENGTH
for the MOMENT

Inspiration for
CAREGIVERS

Lori Hogan

IMAGE

New York

Published in the United States by Image Books, an imprint of the
Crown Publishing Group, a division of Random House, Inc.,
New York.

IMAGE and the Image colophon are registered trademarks of
Random House, Inc.

Cataloging-in-Publication Data is on file with the Library of Congress.

ISBN 978-0-307-88700-9
eISBN 978-0-307-88702-3

Printed in the United States of America

Cover design: Nupoor Gordon
Cover illustration: © Bubaone/iStockphoto

10 9 8 7 6 5 4 3 2 1

First Edition

I humbly dedicate this book to our Heavenly Father, for it was He who gave me inspiration and strength to finish this project; may it honor and glorify Him.

To my loving husband, Paul, for encouraging me to persevere every step of the way. His wisdom and insights enhanced the book, especially when I experienced mental roadblocks. I am blessed beyond measure for his love and support!

To my dear children—Lakelyn, Mickele, Martin, and Jacquelyn—for allowing me to use excerpts of their lives to make my introductions richer. I thank them for their patience and the many nights they had to "fend for themselves" throughout this project.

And I especially dedicate this book to all the family caregivers who may need strength and encouragement as they work through their daily trials. May Strength for the Moment *be a blessing to you all and a celebration of the joys of caregiving!*

Contents

Acknowledgments

I gratefully acknowledge the collaborative efforts of my extraordinary writing team who helped me create *Strength for the Moment*. They not only gave of their time but truly gave of their hearts and souls to make this project a reality.

Jim Beck recognized the need for a book like this and encouraged me to share the inspiring stories of caregivers. He provided humble direction and advice and kept us believing that this book would touch many lives in a meaningful way. I thank him for his unending support, integrity, Scriptural knowledge, and faith.

Melissa Collier was my right hand in preparing the original manuscript. She wrote these stories in the first person so readers could identify with the heart-filled emotions of each caregiver. This book is a reality because of her insightful writing skills. I thank Melissa for her role in making *Strength for the Moment* truly something special.

Larry Novicki, my wonderful father, was one of our main editors. Larry is a retired news editor from the

Omaha World-Herald and has over thirty-five years of editorial experience. He has a keen eye for detail and was snappy in meeting all our deadlines. His involvement meant the world to me, and I thank him from the bottom of my heart!

The Home Instead family of franchise owners, international franchise partners, home office staff, caregivers, business associates, family, friends, and acquaintances graciously opened their hearts to share their caregiving experiences with us. It was inspiring to me, and I am deeply indebted to them all.

The Dilenschneider Group, with special gratitude to Bob Dilenschneider and Joe Tessitore, who proposed *Strength for the Moment* to Doubleday Religion (now Image).

I wish to sincerely thank Image for putting their faith and trust in me to produce a book that will be helpful for many aging parents, their adult children, and special needs families.

Home Instead Senior Care's marketing team assisted with the design and cover of the book. This team has been very influential in the development of our marketing strategies for *Strength for the Moment*.

A big thank-you goes out to my Bible Study Fellowship girlfriends, Sallie Frei, Julie Hillmer, Kim Troia, and Cindy Wofford. These ladies helped me select appropriate Bible verses, crafted meaningful caregiver prayers, and prayed for you, the reader, and every individual who submitted a story. Our hope is that those prayers will give you God's peace, hope, comfort, and encouragement for any caregiving situation.

Introduction

Each year I have the distinct honor of presenting the Caregiver of the Year Award at our Home Instead International Convention. This winner is chosen from among our 65,000 professional caregivers throughout North America. The Caregiver of the Year humbly shares with the audience why she or he loves being a caregiver, then goes on to explain the joy they get from knowing they are making a significant difference in a senior's life and the rewards they reap in return. Usually there is not a dry eye in the house. Being a part of this wonderful ceremony and the process of selecting the Caregiver of the Year has given me an enormous appreciation for what it means to be a caregiver, both the challenges and the rewards this role provides.

This book, *Strength for the Moment*, is my salute to caregivers like you who may go unrecognized for your hard work, compassion, and devotion. Caregivers are truly unsung heroes in their households and communities. My hope is that this book provides you with daily inspiration, strength, and encouragement as you continue to care for your loved one's physical and emotional needs.

God provides for our needs. Our Lord meets us right where we are and gives us just what we need when we ask Him faithfully and believingly. What strength do you need for this moment?

I chose the title *Strength for the Moment* because caregiving situations change from one moment to the next. At any one moment you may be praying for guidance and strength, patience while dealing with family members, wisdom to understand a doctor's instructions, endurance to make it through the evening shift, humor in a difficult or stressful situation, joy in the times of trouble, courage to make tough decisions, one more day to share the gift of life, or encouragement to make it through the next moment and then the next.

I have organized each reading with an introduction, Scripture verse, story, and caregiver prayer. The brief introduction to each entry is based on my own thoughts and experiences. I pray that it gives you some insight into my life and helps to put the focus on lessons we can learn from each story and ultimately on the Lord as our source of strength.

Because Scripture is the living, breathing Word of God and relevant for our lives today, I have included a passage with each story, using the New International Version of the Bible. I encourage you to read these verses in your own Bible. You will find that comparing the passage in a different translation gives God's Word more depth and meaning.

The caregiving stories you are about to read are real and based on the experiences of our Home Instead partners, family members, friends, and other acquaintances. It was not difficult to find people in caregiving roles—they are everywhere. Many do their work quietly and privately not looking for any recognition. More people than I realized are dealing with caregiving issues, and many of them feel alone and overwhelmed. They yearn for comfort and encouragement from others.

The fifty-two stories in this devotional book emphasize the many different emotions that are common among the myriad of caregiving relationships: daughters, sons, spouses, parents, siblings, neighbors, strangers, and professional caregivers. Remarkably, many people told us that just the act of telling or writing their stories was cleansing or therapeutic for them. I was amazed at the many touching stories of love and compassion that family caregivers so willingly shared. I appreciated the genuineness of a daughter struggling to find peace in the midst of a father's Alzheimer's disease. Or the arduous daily routines of a mother with stage IV cancer who finally must accept hospice care. It is my prayer that within these pages you will find new inspiration and a fresh perspective for your caregiving situation.

Finally and very importantly, I have included caregiver prayers meant to bless you and give you God's strength for your every caregiving task. From the very beginning of writing this book, it was my desire to cover it in prayer. My hope is that you feel God's presence and unconditional love as you read these real-life experiences and meditate on God's Word. Thank you for what you do, friend—you are precious in His sight! Enjoy the journey.

May God bless you abundantly,
Lori Hogan

STRENGTH

for the

MOMENT

A DAUGHTER'S HEART

Daylight comes again and I am there.
I search for you among the white hair and blank stares.
Today, you appear anxious and small.
I wonder if you will recognize me at all.
I reach for your hand saying, "Hello, Mother,"
As I introduce myself, "It is Lucy, your daughter."
Your face wrinkles with delight while
I relish this daily gift from God, though slight.
I hold you in my arms and you close your eyes and sigh.
It is all I need this day to get by.
I feed you and care for you,
A daily routine interrupted by something new.
Among the constant jumble of words you speak comes a
    clear
"I could go with you" with a hug you seek.
My heart aches and I comfort you like a mother comforts
    a child.
How I long for my mother to comfort me for a while.

Lucy Novelly
5-14-2004

DENTURES
AND DIGNITY

INTRODUCTION

Some of my friends are being faced with the agonizing decision of whether it is time to put their parents into a nursing home. They are feeling confused, guilty, stressed, and sick to their stomachs. It is heartbreaking because my friends know most parents want to remain in their own homes for as long as possible.

Leviticus tells us we must respect our mother and father, "rise in the presence of the aged, show respect for the elderly and revere your God." I believe this passage means not only to literally rise in the presence of the elderly but also to rise to the responsibility of taking care of our parents' needs. Simply providing new dentures or a hearing aid can mean the difference between home and a nursing home, as the following story illustrates.

INSPIRATIONAL VERSE

Be shepherds of God's flock that is under your care, serving as overseers—not because you must, but because you are willing, as God wants you to be; not greedy for money, but eager to serve; not lording it over those entrusted to you, but being examples to the flock. And when the Chief Shepherd appears, you will receive the crown of glory that will never fade away.

1 PETER 5:2—4

MESSAGE

When Dad was ninety years old, his neighbor told me it was time for us to take him to a nursing home. Why? He couldn't hear, couldn't see, and wasn't eating right.

It turned out the neighbor was right about Dad's condition. He couldn't hear well. His vision was not as clear as it once had been. But instead of putting him in a nursing home, my wife, Saundra, and I welcomed him into our home. We bought him a hearing aid. A nursing home couldn't cure his poor vision, but cataract surgery did. He wasn't eating right because his teeth were no good, so we got him dentures.

How many times do we assume the challenges of aging are unsolvable and permanent? At what point do we begin to chalk things up to old age, about which nothing can be done? We never thought of Dad as a problem or a burden but as a human being who was not yet done living.

Dad had always been an excellent provider. He found great dignity at the end of a hard day's work. Memories of how proud he was to care for himself and his family shaped the man and father I became. Regardless of age or health, I still believed that he would find dignity at the end of a hard day's work. Saundra and I had him do as much on his own as possible, and that made him feel good about himself, even in the smallest way.

Dad made his bed, folded clothes, cared for the dogs, fixed lunch, watched TV, dressed himself, and counted his money. We made sure he washed his hair, brushed his teeth, and wore clean clothes, all so that he could keep looking and feeling good.

We rejected the idea that, because he was weak, he had to stay weak and fragile. We helped him start a regular exercise routine. He came to believe in the use it or lose it principle—that weakness and senility can be delayed or defeated with exercise and mental stimulation.

He was soon riding a stationary bike two miles each day and lifting three-pound weights. Dad was also able to enjoy walks with the dogs. Being able to walk with only a cane gave Dad a huge sense of accomplishment.

Saundra created a system to keep challenging his mind. She used a lazy Susan on the kitchen table to keep Dad's food and medicine, and she attached to it Post-it notes with mind-stimulating questions: "Who is the governor?" "Who is the president?" The answers were always on the back sides of the notes, and Dad would "cheat" by hiding the notes among the ketchup and salt and pepper shakers. He loved outwitting Saundra. It became dinnertime amusement when he searched through his cheat sheets to find the answers.

Dad was a joy and a gift, not someone just to be taken care of. Did keeping him active and expecting him to contribute to his own care improve the quality and length of his life? We think so. But whether it did or not, sharing his final seven years was an unexpected gift. I learned to know, love, and appreciate Dad all the more. He found dignity by working hard until he died at age ninety-seven.

Bob Darrah

"We never thought of Dad as a problem or a burden but as a human being who was not yet done living."

CAREGIVER'S PRAYER

Chief Shepherd, you are the Great Provider,

Thank you for entrusting me with the care of my parents. Provide me with creative ways in which to keep my parents active and independent for as long as possible—engaging their minds, bodies and spirits. Let me satisfy their needs in a way that displays the utmost dignity.

BABY SENT FROM GOD

INTRODUCTION

Six months after our first child was born, I had emergency surgery because of an ectopic pregnancy. It was a traumatic event for Paul and me, but I knew I was going to be just fine. Was God trying to capture my attention? As I lay in the hospital for four days, I asked the Lord what He was wanting to teach me.

I was very impressed with two thoughts. One: I was wasting too much God-given time on things of little importance. I needed to change my ways and engage in those activities that had more Eternal worth and value. Two: Human life is so very precious no matter how tiny, such as an embryo, or how old, such as the elderly or frail. Do not take life for granted; life has meaning at any phase, and we are to appreciate and protect it.

The following story of Sharon, a woman with frontal-lobe dementia, is a beautiful example of pairing desires of the heart with acts of meaningful service for others.

Sharon's caregiver was motivated to satisfy her friend's desire and bring faith, hope, and purpose back into her life. God provided Sharon with a beautiful memory that brought her tears of joy and a satisfied heart.

INSPIRATIONAL VERSE

"For I know the plans I have for you," declares the Lord, "plans to prosper you and not harm you, plans to give you hope and a future."

JEREMIAH 29:11

MESSAGE

Shortly after beginning my journey at Home Instead Senior Care, I received a phone call from a woman who was lost and needed our help immediately. Her name was Sharon, and the fear and anguish in her voice shook me to my core. Sharon had frontal-lobe dementia, and it was clear that she needed much more care than she was receiving. I began to pray that God would help me find the perfect caregiver to help Sharon.

Cindy was one of my newest caregivers, but something in my heart made me believe that she could make Sharon's life better. Sharon and Cindy became fast friends, and their friendship provided stability that Sharon had been lacking. Since frontal-lobe dementia does not affect memory, Sharon was able to share remarkable stories about her life in New York City as a director of nursing and a renowned medical practitioner. Cindy also learned that Sharon had never married or had children of her own.

During trips to the zoo, bike rides, and walks, Sharon told Cindy about how nursing had provided her with a great sense of connection to the human spirit. She still yearned to be part of something and to feel the acclaim she'd once known so well. As a nurse, she understood how important it is to stay active and engaged. However, as her illness grew worse and her fear of the outside world increased, her connection to the human spirit waned. Cindy's determination to find a way for Sharon to feel connected to the world beyond her disease grew stronger every day. One afternoon Sharon lit up as she mentioned that she used to volunteer at the nearby Child Saving Institute, rocking babies in the nursery.

Cindy was as excited as Sharon at the possibility of her volunteering, and we all prayed that this could be the answer to Sharon's heartache. I made a phone call, only to learn that her request had been denied. Cindy was heartbroken and adamantly replied, "You have to do something!" The truth is that we both wanted, if only for one day, for Sharon to feel her purpose again. Like Sharon's, my hope, faith, and purpose have waned at times. I connected with her feeling of being lost and waiting to be found.

By coincidence—no, make that Divine intervention—my mother owns a home day care and was eager to help Sharon. After all necessary approvals were granted, we surprised Sharon with a field trip to my mother's home. I prayed that I was doing the right thing. Sharon was greeted with big smiles from all the children. My mother had a rocking chair waiting for Sharon and asked if she'd like to have a seat. She then put a baby into Sharon's arms. The tiny baby instantly snuggled into Sharon's neck and did not make a noise for an hour, as if he had been instructed by the Lord. Sharon sat back and tears streamed down her cheeks. She softly said, "I'm so happy."

These moments affirm for me that I am exactly where I am supposed to be at this point in my life. I am truly blessed to be a part of something so much greater than I am. After we prayed relentlessly for weeks, in the blink of an eye, hope filled a hopeless face and dignity returned to a woman who had been stripped of so much by an ugly disease. We witnessed a baby sent from God, to give worth to a woman who so greatly needed another human spirit to help her regain her faith, hope, and purpose.

Megan Mueller

> "*Like Sharon's, my hope,*
> *faith, and purpose have waned*
> *at times. I connected with her*
> *feeling of being lost and*
> *waiting to be found.*"

CAREGIVER'S PRAYER

Constant Companion,

You are the giver of life and all that is good. You tell us to make the desires of our hearts known to you, and you will fulfill them. Continue to shower me with joy and satisfaction whether I am caring for an elder or an infant. Empower me to make a difference in that person's life. Show me the best way to care for their needs and let me rely on your guidance and strength to accomplish this task. I am thankful that you have given me the desire to take care of others.

THE LADDER OF LOVE

INTRODUCTION

I believe we are called to honor and care for our parents until their very last days of life. God commands us to honor thy father and thy mother in Exodus 20:12. He felt this commandment was so important that He wrote it with His own finger on stone.

This story is a beautiful example of a daughter's struggle to keep her mother at home. She likens going through the stages of her mother's Alzheimer's disease to descending a ladder rung by rung.

INSPIRATIONAL VERSE

Give proper recognition to those widows who are really in need. But if a widow has children or grandchildren, these should learn first of all to put their religion into practice by caring for their own family and so repaying

their parents and grandparents, for this is
pleasing to God.

I TIMOTHY 5:3-4

MESSAGE

Mom was only seventy-one, in great health, fun-loving,
vivacious, and outgoing when she was diagnosed with
Alzheimer's disease. Strange as this may sound, that diagnosis was a relief! She and we knew something was
wrong, so we were all relieved to learn that there was a
medical reason for her forgetfulness.

Mom had enough wits about her to worry that others might think she was just dumb or forgetful. In fact,
she proudly added the "news" of her diagnosis to her
annual Christmas letter.

I learned to view Mom's Alzheimer's as though it was
a two-sided ladder, with each rung representing a year.
When life was normal, Mom advanced in age up one side
of the ladder, but with Alzheimer's she began to move
down the other. This simple imagery allowed me talk
about her situation in ways that really helped me communicate what was happening.

When Mom "turned six" on the back side of the
ladder, my granddaughter, Jaiden, was also six. Mom
loved Jaiden, but suddenly this innocent six-year-old
irritated Mom. She would scold, pick on, and blame
Jaiden whenever something was missing or broken.
This behavior was surprising and frustrating to me

until I caught a TV program about young girls fighting. That's when I realized that my mom was just a little girl too.

At "five years" Mom discovered boys and developed a crush on Ed, who happened also to live in the memory support unit. She talked about him constantly. She would primp and fuss to make sure that he noticed her. Ed was married and his wife visited him daily, but that didn't matter. Mom was convinced it was just his mother! Mom always did have an eye for the good-looking men!

When Mom "turned three" I moved her into my home. It seemed such a waste to be paying all that money for her to live elsewhere when she still needed me to be with her each day. By now Mom couldn't entertain herself. Like most three-year-olds, she demanded my full attention—following me from room to room, staring impatiently at me when I was on the phone, and pouting when I didn't have time to play with her.

Luckily, I discovered an activity that kept Mom's attention. Just like every three-year-old, Mom liked to sort! And when I moved her into my home, I brought her rather large collection of costume jewelry along. It turned out to be the perfect activity! She would sit and sort for hours. Item after item got a close inspection before she would look for the exact match. It was perfect for Mom and perfect for me!

Seeing Mom happy made me happy, but it also made me sad. It was at that point that I knew I had to let go of the Mom I once knew. She was gone. I leaned heavily upon my faith and prayers. It felt as if I was mourning my mother's death while caring for the child she had become.

At "two" things got harder. I should have known—they don't call them the *terrible twos* for nothing! Mom's vocabulary shrank. Her temper tantrums worsened. She became jealous of my husband. She would meet me at the door pointing and glaring at him. She would mutter and mumble about "him" without end. I explained to her that Jeff was my husband, that I loved him, and that she needed to be nice to him. But like a two-year-old, she rejected everything that she couldn't understand.

Fortunately, I was blessed by marrying an extremely patient and kind man. He knew it was the disease talking, not my mother. It didn't matter—it still hurt! It still *looked* like my mom. It still *sounded* like my mom. It was next to impossible not to respond. I started to take out my frustrations on my family. I cried—a lot! Mom loved it when Jeff and I would fight. She'd make comments like "What is *he* doing here? I thought we got rid of him!"

It felt as if I was losing my family. Yet somehow I had to face reality. I knew that I could no longer handle this alone. I prayed for God's guidance about the difficult decision just ahead.

I live by the motto Look, see, and tell the truth. I didn't have the time, mental capacity, or energy to give my husband, my children, or my grandchildren what they needed. I wasn't taking care of myself.

Finally, I moved Mom back into an Alzheimer's

care center. It was the right decision, but it was also the most difficult thing I've ever done. It felt like abandoning my baby! What would she do without me? What if she got scared? What if she needed me? What if no one knew what she was trying to say? What if she thought I didn't love her anymore?

Mom is now around "eighteen months" on her age ladder. She babbles and uses her hands to try to tell me what's going on. Her face lights up with delight when I come to visit. She blurts out one of the few words she has left. "*Really? Really?*" she stammers. Mom is in diapers most of the time and has trouble keeping her balance. In most every way, she's a toddler.

I bathe her (she loves playing in the water!), fix her hair, or go with her for ice cream. My favorite time now is cuddling on the couch and reading Bible stories to her. She just loves hearing my voice, but it's the sound of my voice, not the words and stories, that provides solace and acceptance.

I try to give her everything I can. I want to take care of her the way she took care of me. When I tuck her in at night and tell her I love her, I'm almost overcome with joy. She just smiles and in a timid little voice says, "I lo-lo-lo-love you too." The disease changed everything, but there's one thing that it can't take away from me: She is still my mom and I love her with all my heart.

LuAnn Anglo

"*It was a two-sided ladder,
with each rung representing a
year. . . . Mom advanced in
age up one side of the ladder,
but with Alzheimer's she began
to move down the other.*"

CAREGIVER'S PRAYER

God of Abraham, Isaac, and Jacob,

When you called me to care for my mother I never dreamed it would be this difficult. Please open my eyes to opportunities that surround me to stimulate and interact with her throughout the day. Help me to see that spending time with my mother is a privilege and a blessing, and not a burden.

THE BOILING POT

INTRODUCTION

Some days I wish I had superpowers like Superwoman so I could save time by flying to appointments. Or I wish I could be like the Energizer Bunny, which keeps going and going and going, so I could accomplish a hundred tasks in one day and not feel like I was always lagging behind.

Raising four children in our home made life hectic most of the time. Is there a Scripture passage or phrase that has truly helped you throughout your busy life? I have two quotes that I rely on to this day: "This too shall pass" and "I can do everything through Him who gives me strength," which have been two of my lifelines. I don't know how many times I said those words from when the kids were in diapers, during the terrible twos, while I was refereeing sibling quarrels until they were well into their teenage years. Life gets tough! But God got me through each trial. I did not always smell like a rose, mind you, but I had faith and trust in God's promises. When we are dependent upon the Lord for our strength, He will get us to where He wants us to be.

Who among us hasn't at some time felt frustration that boils over as it did for Melissa in this story?

> ### INSPIRATIONAL VERSE
> Whatever you do, work at it with all your heart, as working for the Lord, not for men. . . . It is the Lord Christ you are serving.
>
> COLOSSIANS 3:23–24

MESSAGE

I cried today. It happened somewhere between changing the diapers of my one-year-old, Annie, and those of my elderly mother-in-law, Carol; getting them down for naps; and rushing to fold clothes while they slept. There was no more holding it in. No more putting on a happy face. No more pretending that this was how I wanted my life to be.

Laundry basket in hand, I simply sat on the middle steps and the tears began to fall. Not usually one to let my emotions get the better of me, I surprised even myself. Why today? It was a day like any other—chores, doctors' appointments, diapers, naps, and baths. I couldn't really put my finger on exactly why I was crying; I just felt like a pot, sitting there and boiling over.

Silly, but as I sat and looked at the basket of clothes, I suddenly yearned for my husband to see me in something other than sweatpants and a sweatshirt. I wanted to rush upstairs, shower, curl my hair, and look pretty for Jack when he came home tonight. There on the stairwell, my mind raced as I thought of who I could call to come over and sit with the "girls" tonight. Jack and I could have dinner out, a glass of wine, a real conversation.

The tears fell faster with the realization that no one would be able to come on such short notice. It was already late and I needed to get dinner started. I told myself to get busy and quit being silly; after all, I was blessed with a beautiful home, daughter, husband, and a wonderful family.

My tears had dampened the freshly folded whites. With equally dampened spirits, I accidentally let go and watched the basket tumble to the bottom of the stairs, where I let it lie. It would still be there tomorrow, and I had too much to do to worry about it then. I wiped my final tears on the sleeve of my sweatshirt and started dinner.

Later, as I was rocking Annie to sleep, I found myself whispering an absurd promise: "Angel, I'll never put you through this." On my way down to Jack, I stopped in Carol's room, kissed her forehead, and said, "I know this isn't your fault."

In the morning, I found the basket on top of the stairs. Laundry neatly folded. No note. No questions. None needed. His simple gesture said all it needed to say; I wasn't in this alone.

Melissa Collier

"I just felt like a pot, sitting there and boiling over."

CAREGIVER'S PRAYER

Heavenly Savior,

Thank you for comforting me when I am feeling down and alone. Help me not to wish these days away but to turn to you for guidance, patience, and love. Give me your mighty power to complete the many tasks that fill my day, and joy and peace in my heart knowing that I am doing the best that I can do with your help.

SELFLESS SERVICE

INTRODUCTION

Back in the year 2000, Paul and I flew to Japan for our first overseas business trip. We were going to be gone for about a week and needed to enlist help from family and friends to take care of our four children while we traveled. Getting the kids to school, practices, games, and lessons was part of the challenge, mingled with meals, baths, and bedtime. It took quite a bit of planning, and I felt nervous that everything would not go smoothly while we were away. Paul reminded me that we had the right people slotted for the right tasks, which allowed me to relax and enjoy with confidence my green tea and sushi.

Our travels now frequently take us around the world. The children are growing up and are more able to take care of themselves, but I am still deeply grateful that we have family to be there when we need them. When we give selfless service to others, it returns to us twofold with blessings of love and gratitude, as illustrated in Mary's experience with her family.

INSPIRATIONAL VERSE

"Be strong and courageous, and do the work. Do not be afraid or discouraged, for the Lord God, my God, is with you. He will not fail you or forsake you until all the work for the service of the temple of the Lord is finished."

I CHRONICLES 28:20

MESSAGE

When I unexpectedly became a divorced, working mother, my friends and family rallied around me and helped me raise my children. I didn't have to ask. My family and friends could see that I needed them, and they jumped in with both feet to do whatever was required. They had no expectation of future repayment; they were simply honored and happy to be there in my time of need.

As my own mother began to age and required more care, I understood. It was not obligation or expectation but love. Caregiving cannot be done alone. My family quickly learned that it takes a caring community to raise happy and healthy children. That same community is needed to care for happy elderly parents. Living with Mom wasn't the best option for her personality or mine, but I wanted to be nearby. Newly single, I bought the home next door to Mom so that I could be there when she needed me. She was the best neighbor I have ever had.

I learned that caregiving is far more than doing the

necessary daily tasks, such as cooking meals, mowing lawns, or cleaning house; it is the accumulation of offering a loving touch, exchanging knowing looks, and foreseeing the needs of others before they even know to ask for help. Being a caregiver has changed me; it has allowed me to look deeper into people's souls than I was able to before. However, being the recipient of family care also changed me; it opened my heart more than I believed possible. It is through an open heart that love flows freely.

Caregiving, like parenting, is not give-and-take. Successful parents and caregivers open their hearts to pain, vulnerability, and hard work. They do whatever it takes and see it not as a burden but rather as an honor to be involved in the upbringing of a child or the care of an aging parent.

And, like parents, caregivers often feel overwhelmed and helpless. It is terribly frustrating to know that at some point, no matter what you do, the result is often the same. When you are in the midst of difficult situations, caregiving and parenting both seem like unflattering roles. Why put ourselves through the grief and suffering? Why keep fighting battles that appear to be already lost? Because after the grief, sacrifice, and frustration wane, being a caregiver is the best role ever. Love and dedication carry more weight and keep us stable in otherwise tumultuous circumstances. Our emotions can carry us away, but they also keep us grounded.

One of Mom's hospice nurses taught us all an invaluable lesson. She said not to wait. To ask the tough questions, say what is on our minds, and forgive one another before it is too late. She was right: Knowing that everything had been said and that none of us was holding anything back filled our hearts with love. A full heart understands that death isn't always loss; it's merely a change of our loved one's presence in our life.

That is not to say that every person faced with the role of a caregiver has the same skills. I have learned through divorce and the aging and illness of my mother that families, like communities, need to play to their strengths. Every community needs an accountant, a doctor, a carpenter, a businessman to do what every successful team, town, or business does: divide and conquer. Assign tasks to those who are best suited for each job. Don't put the brother who is always broke and looking for work in charge of the finances just because he has plenty of free time. Don't ask the sister who hates to cook to be in charge of meals just because she has a nice kitchen. Put the cook at the stove, hand the checkbook to the accountant, give the hammer to the carpenter, and work together to get the job done.

There is no easy road, no easy way, no easy answer. One good day can be followed by an avalanche of bad days. And, to be honest, at times my faith wavered. The days when I lacked belief in God were the darkest. Without the belief that there is a presence greater than myself to help me through the daily trials, life just didn't make sense. But I learned to choose not to be angry and just trust that God was there for me and my family. I learned that closing my heart is never the answer. Keeping an open heart to God in the face of adversity is the key that unlocks the power of selfless service to others.

Mary Alexander

> "*Because after the grief, sacrifice, and frustration wane, being a caregiver is the best role ever.*"

CAREGIVER'S PRAYER

Servant Lord,

You are the perfect example of a humble servant. Teach us to serve others with love and compassion the way you selflessly served your people while on earth. Reveal to us those in our family and caring community who have special skills so they can efficiently supply the proper care for our loved ones. You graciously bless our selfless service to others in many seen and unforeseen ways. Thank you for your tender heart toward me.

JUST BREATHE

INTRODUCTION

Years ago I received a devastating phone call telling me that four of my cousins were involved in a fatal car accident. Mary, who had been driving, was seriously injured, requiring the Jaws of Life to free her from the wreckage. Her daughter, Katherine, was sitting behind her and endured only a broken collarbone. Mary's sister, Bobbee, was sitting in the passenger seat and suffered lacerations and broken bones. But Bobbee's daughter, Ila, was killed in the head-on collision. She was only twelve years old. She suffered massive internal injuries that left her lifeless at the scene.

Shock and denial were my initial reactions to this horrific news. I could not believe this had happened to my cousins. I could hardly breathe. Their lives were changed forever from that very moment. A young life of promise and hope was gone in an instant. How were they to cope? What was God's plan in all this?

These were some of the same questions and emotions

that ran through the minds of Erin and Steve when they encountered their family crisis.

INSPIRATIONAL VERSE

Trust in the Lord with all your heart
and lean not on your own understanding;
in all your ways acknowledge him,
and he will make your paths straight.

PROVERBS 3:5–6

MESSAGE

Life can change very quickly. Sometimes so quickly that our minds and hearts struggle to keep up. Regardless of whether the news is good or bad, the sudden impact of a totally new reality is most often met with disbelief. Perhaps God gives us those initial moments of "I can't believe this is happening" as a means to absorb the shock and brace ourselves for whatever happiness or sadness lies ahead.

Sometimes, however, our hearts or minds get stuck and we aren't able to accept that this new reality belongs to us. My husband, Steve, was a classic example of denial after finding out that his father, Jack, was full of cancer. They had been on their annual fishing trip at the same spot they had been to every year for thirty years when Steve first noticed his dad wasn't quite himself. From that moment, the events unfolded quickly.

How could they have been fishing one beautiful June day and Jack be so sick the next? It was odd that

Jack had suggested they head back to camp early, but at the time Steve thought nothing of it. From his tent Steve could see into his dad's camper, and he saw his father leaning over the bed, coughing so violently that Steve decided to take him to the hospital. The doctors concluded it was a bad case of pneumonia and transferred Jack to his local hospital for further care. Again, Steve thought nothing of it because his dad was young and strong. No one, least of all Steve, could have predicted that, ten days after catching his last fish, Jack would be dying.

On the eighth day, it was time to discuss either putting Jack on a ventilator or putting him in hospice care. I had to explain to Steve what hospice care entailed because he, like many people, didn't know. After giving what I thought was a thorough explanation, I looked over to find a very angry husband. He was certain that I couldn't know what I was talking about, and he was very upset that I was so matter-of-fact about it.

His emotions were blocking out the truth. So rather than defend myself, I simply tried again. This time, I took a less clinical approach and explained how the hospice staff would administer medication to help Steve's father relax and make him comfortable during his final days. Jack's breathing had become painful, so the idea of his being comfortable seemed to reach beyond the wall of avoidance that Steve had constructed.

Still, he turned to me and said, "Fine, but you have to go tell him." Jack's only question was "Is this the end?" to which I answered "Yes." He then spoke his last audible words: "I just want to be able to breathe again."

As we drove to the hospice center the next morning, Steve started talking about how the medication should be working by now and that Dad should be feeling better. "Maybe he will be up and at it today," he said. I'll never forget looking over at Steve as he spoke, knowing he honestly believed that might be the outcome. I thought, Wow, did I do such a poor job explaining hospice to him? Denial was a river pumping through my husband's veins, and it broke my heart to tell him that Dad would not be "up and at it" and that, instead, this would likely be the day Jack would die.

God granted us a few more hours with Jack, which allowed Steve time to brace himself for the inevitable. Steve's mind may have initially rejected the truth, but his love for Jack was far stronger than his denial. Steve may not have wanted to hear that hospice was the right decision, but his heart was listening, and it understood.

Jack was able to take his final breath on his own. It was beautiful.

Erin Albers

"*Steve's mind may have initially rejected the truth, but his love for Jack was far stronger than his denial.*"

CAREGIVER'S PRAYER

Omnipotent God,

Life does not always go as we plan. Help me to understand your ways, because I am having a hard time making sense of my situation. Help me to move from denying my circumstances to putting my trust in you during this difficult time of confusion and sadness. Build up my faith, Father, so that I may confidently accept your wise plan for me.

THE ONE WITH
THE SMILE

INTRODUCTION

One thing I always admired about my grandma Damrow was her sense of humor. One time when we were visiting Grandma in the hospital, she was just waking up from surgery and looked quite confused. She started to feel her stomach in a circular motion and asked, "Am I pregnant?" We all laughed so hard, and she smiled as if to make it an intentional joke. She probably remembered being in the hospital when she was delivering her three children many, many years ago and truly thought that was the reason she was there now. I think my grandma frequently used humor to cover up her dementia; nonetheless, we were pleased to see that she still possessed a great sense of humor at the age of ninety.

Humor is a great way to lighten the mood or to lift someone's spirit, as Karyn has learned in many of her caregiving situations.

INSPIRATIONAL VERSE
A cheerful look brings joy to the heart,
and good news gives health to the bones.

PROVERBS 15:30

MESSAGE

As a professional caregiver for elderly, ill, and sometimes dying clients, I have felt every emotion possible for my clients and their families. I hesitate even to call them clients because, although I am getting paid for helping them, they all quickly become friends. I often feel like one of the family. Knowing that each day I'm really making a difference is a joy.

That's not to say that every situation is easy, but I honestly love my job as a professional caregiver in Brisbane, Australia. I never quite know what each day will bring, but regardless of the situation, the care for someone who needs it is at stake, and I take that very seriously. At the office, I'm known as "the one with the smile" or "the one with the laugh" when clients call to request me for an assignment. It makes me happy that what they most remember about me is my laugh or my smile. That is the only recognition I need to know that I have touched someone in a positive way.

My recipe for success has been to go into every home with a smile and the intention to lift the spirits of those who live there. Even in the most dire situations, something as simple as a smile can make a huge difference.

I try to have fun with my clients, so I often sing and joke with them, which most really respond to. One time, I was watching *Mary Poppins* with one of my Alzheimer's clients, and I was singing along (loudly) and couldn't tell if she liked it or not. Jokingly, I told her that if she didn't like my singing she could ask me to leave. Without missing a beat, she promptly stood, walked me to her front door, and said, "Let me show you to the gate, my darling." It is these moments that I cherish the most. To find such a sense of humor intact despite age or illness left me amazed. If she had been well, I just know we would have been brilliant friends.

Not every assignment has a happy ending, and not everything can be cured with a smile. Another of my long-term clients had a heart attack while I was caring for her. I accompanied her to the hospital, where I stayed until she passed away. Unfortunately, her family lived outside Brisbane and was not able to get there in time. I was able to provide them details of her last hours, how she became anxious before slipping into a coma and how I sang to her to relieve some of her anxiety. They were comforted to know that I had been at their mum's side until the end.

I've come to appreciate how difficult a decision it is for families to hire outside help to care for their mums and dads. Feelings of guilt and worry overwhelm some families, while others can more easily admit they need the assistance. The parent or relative may be the one I am providing physical care for, but I consider the entire family as clients. Bringing in outside help is an adjustment at first, but honestly, I think most families are glad once they've made the decision to do so. My goal is to give the family peace of mind that their mums, dads, aunts, or uncles will receive the level of care they deserve.

Recently, a client called in and told the owner of our company that "Karyn is the joy of my old age," but the truth is, I get so much more from this job than I could possibly ever give. It is true what they say—that when you do what you love, it hardly feels like work at all.

Karyn McLennan

"My recipe for success has been to go into every home with a smile and the intention to lift the spirits of those who live there."

CAREGIVER'S PRAYER

Blessed Father,

Thank you for the joy I experience when I am taking care of the seniors in my life. You tell us that it is more blessed to give than to receive, and I believe that with my whole heart. Help me to always have a giving spirit, warm smile, and tender heart to share with others.

POTTER'S WHEELCHAIR

INTRODUCTION

I often wonder why God allows afflictions to take over our bodies so that we are no longer capable of movement or speech. Or why some brains are not capable of processing information properly or some personalities are wildly distorted.

I remind myself that, if all of us were perfect, we would not need one another, or God for that matter. He wants us to love one another, show compassion and mercy, and to be His hands and feet on this earth to serve others.

The Lord gives us many opportunities to serve others if we would just open our eyes and heed God's quiet nudges and tugs on our hearts. Sarah obeys His call by reaching out to one of His people in need. The blessings are abundant when we listen and obey.

....

INSPIRATIONAL VERSE

Yet, O Lord, you are our Father.
We are the clay, you are the potter;
we are all the work of your hand.

ISAIAH 64:8

....

MESSAGE

I have known Sherri for over twenty years. We met through a philanthropy that we both supported. At first we were acquaintances who saw each other a couple times a month at meetings. In 1998 my friend was diagnosed with multiple sclerosis.

Our group rallied around Sherri and her family by providing meals, cleaning house, and running errands. We even had a community benefit to help raise money for a wheelchair-accessible van. Initially, I viewed Sherri as one of our philanthropy projects, a person I could reach out a temporary hand to help every now and then.

But God began to work on me as I attended a women's Bible study called Bible Study Fellowship (BSF). Through this, He began to change my heart to have His compassion and love; He changed my eyes to see with grace, humility, tenderness; He changed my priorities and slowed down my pace.

I was soon passionate about sharing the Gospel with others and invited Sherri to attend BSF. She accepted and became a committed student, rarely missing a class in spite of the effort it took for her to come.

Sherri and I have been studying the Word together for over ten years. Over this time she has become my sister and my friend, no longer a "project" but a person I love.

I discovered that when I serve with a "project" mentality, it is more of a "good deed," serving out of a sense of "duty." But when I seek the Lord and He gives me opportunities to serve, the result is a double blessing.

Despite her progressive physical decline due to MS, Sherri remains upbeat and positive because her hope is in the Lord. She witnesses Christ to her caregivers, family, and friends. Sherri's ability to memorize Scripture is amazing. She often blesses me and others with the right verse at the right time.

Through Sherri, I truly see the Lord provide. He shows up regularly to offer what is needed:

- Caregivers who come to her home to get her ready for the day, run errands, and help with housework
- Friends who read her mail, pay her bills, or drop in for a visit, coffee, or lunch

It is awesome to see the many ways God provides for my friend.

Some days, I get angry and frustrated that God has not answered my prayer for healing. It's difficult to watch my friend's health decline. She is currently a paraplegic, and her eyesight is all but gone. She wears a catheter and is bound to a wheelchair.

It breaks my heart that Sherri can't see her athletic

son score a touchdown or make the winning basket for his team. But others give her a play-by-play of the game, and her son knows when Mom is there. For her, that is enough.

Sherri has taught me so much:

- To view the glass of life as half full, not half empty.
- To focus on what you can do with excellence instead of sitting in self-pity and depression over what you cannot do.
- To make the most of your God-given gifts and talents. Currently, Sherri cannot walk or see, but she does *listen* and pray.
- To ask for help when you need it. It is a blessing for others to come alongside.

If she didn't have MS, Sherri and I would probably still be just acquaintances meeting once a month at a philanthropy meeting. I am sad that my friend suffers with this disease, yet I see how God has used her wheelchair as His potter's wheel.

Above all, Sherri has taught me what it means to be a true friend: someone who gives not because they "have to" but because they delight in giving, serving out of love instead of guilt, having the freedom to say "I can't today" and hearing "No problem, I'll call someone else."

God's economy is that of "double blessings," and I always leave Sherri's home feeling encouraged. Although she cannot physically walk beside me, she certainly has come alongside me to encourage, pray, and speak truth into my life. For this, I am grateful. Multiple sclerosis may be robbing her physical body, but it certainly can't steal her soul. The greatest thing I can do for Sherri is run the race of life with her. We are not giving up, not quitting in spite of the distance, but putting our hope in God, which renews our strength.

As Sherri's friend, I can offer my hands to serve, whether by emptying her catheter bag, driving her customized van, or giving her game updates. I can laugh with her, cry with her, hold her hand, and give her a hug. I can call, drive her to our meetings, or stop in for a cup of coffee. I can pray with her and offer her hope and encouragement.

Sarah Nordlund

> "I am sad that my friend suffers with this disease, yet I see how God has used her wheelchair as His potter's wheel."

CAREGIVER'S PRAYER

Master Artist, Creator of Hope,

Thank you for your sovereign plan. It is humbling to see how you take our earthly afflictions and give us strength. I pray that I may see the person in front of me not as an obstacle to get around but rather as a person to love and serve. Thank you for weaving the lives of people together to make a beautiful tapestry that enriches our relationship with others and ultimately blesses our relationship with you, O Lord.

CHANGING PERSPECTIVES

INTRODUCTION

I have always wanted to learn how to knit, so one day I asked Paul's grandma Manhart to teach me. I intently watched every move she made, but when it was my turn to knit, purl, cast on, and cast off, I failed miserably. Grandma patiently kept working with me. I started to get so discouraged that I plopped down in front of her in defeat. As I looked up at her clicking needles, the lightbulb went on. I'm left-handed, so seeing her knit the opposite way made sense to me. The look on Grandma's face made me laugh. She probably thought this poor girl was hopeless. Seeing her knit from a different perspective gave me a greater understanding of the task at hand.

Tim had two different experiences caring for his parents—one through the eyes of a teenager and one through the eyes of a young adult. Maturity changed Tim's perspective, and he gained a greater appreciation for the time he had with his parents.

INSPIRATIONAL VERSE

Create in me a pure heart, O God,
and renew a steadfast spirit within me.
Do not cast me from your presence
or take your Holy Spirit from me.
Restore to me the joy of your salvation
and grant me a willing spirit, to sustain me.

PSALM 51:10–12

MESSAGE

It is very interesting how your perspective changes based on your phase in life. I was eighteen when my mom passed at the age of fifty-two after a yearlong battle with cancer. Being a typical teenager, I remember feeling frustrated because I was "forced" to spend time with my mother. Family responsibilities took time away from hanging out with my friends.

As most teenagers do, I believed the world revolved around my wants and needs. That was until I was a senior in high school and my mother was diagnosed with ovarian cancer. She was fifty-one at the time, and I remember initially thinking that God couldn't possibly take a mother of eight away from her family in her prime.

Mom underwent twelve months of chemo treatments back when they didn't have all the antinausea drugs. The first few treatments wore her down both physically and mentally. We knew Mom was in for a long fight.

We received large amounts of support from the community and friends, but ultimately the majority of the responsibility fell on the family. My high school graduation was the first time Mom went out in public with a wig, which was an emotional milestone for her. Mom was a strong lady and was able to continue running the household until the last few months of her treatment. The majority of the caregiving she needed up to this point had been encouragement and rides to and from the chemo treatments.

The final months became more difficult for everyone involved. My personal caregiving became more physical: assisting Mom to move around and in many cases carrying her up the stairs to bed. I remember her taking rest breaks while walking from the car to the house and discussing what this would eventually mean to the family. I also remember the times I helped my mother in public and feeling self-conscious about what others thought. As I matured, I viewed having done all this as a badge of honor, and would not have changed being there with her for the world.

After Mom passed, Dad was never the same. He struggled with heart problems for the last three years of his life before passing at the age of sixty-three, and I believe that in actuality he died of a broken heart. During his illness, I was in my late twenties, married, with one child and another on the way, and I had a totally different view on life and death. Caregiving for my father was very time-consuming and took many forms. Among eight grown children, there was plenty of input on a care plan. The majority of the caregiving was provided by a few of us because several of our siblings lived out of town. Caring for an aging parent and carrying on a healthy marriage was a struggle. Fortunately, my wife loved to help care for my dad.

In many ways, taking care of Dad was more stressful than it had been with Mom, not only because of the frequency of his needs but because of the decisions that had to be made regarding his treatment. I have to be honest and say resentment toward the out-of-town siblings crept into the picture. It is very hard to get consensus among eight kids, but when some are out of town it is nearly impossible. When decisions were made and subsequently second-guessed by siblings who were not involved day to day, it put a heavy burden on the few of us dealing with the hands-on care.

Later in life I realized the gift that I had been given, that we had all been given, which was time with both our parents before they passed. The life lessons learned through caring for them during their final moments have come to mean more and more to me as I've gotten older. After a few years, memories of my mother changed from the sick, frail woman I cared for to the vibrant, social woman she was before she became ill. And the sadness of Dad in his final minutes, with all his children around him at home, has been replaced by memories of the times I spent with him watching a baseball game or talking about parenthood. (I certainly wish I had that opportunity now!) The struggles eventually fade away, and the good memories and their lasting impact on your life are what matters. We all grow from our experiences.

Tim Connelly

"*Later in life I realized the gift that I had been given, that we had all been given, which was time with both our parents before they passed.*"

CAREGIVER'S PRAYER

Sustaining Lord,

It's hard to watch my parents decline in health. I ask you to give me strength during difficult caregiving situations and protect me from discouragement. Give me a willing spirit to see things from different perspectives so I may grow from my caregiving experiences and ultimately come closer to you, Lord.

MY NEXT VISIT

INTRODUCTION

Paul and I had the distinct honor of having dinner with the prime minister of Australia while visiting our international franchise partners Sarah and Martin Warner. While we were getting dressed for this big event, I received an e-mail from our daughter Mickele telling us that our son, Marty, had just broken his arm jumping off Grandma's trampoline with his snowboard on his feet. (Yes, I said *snowboard*.) She went on to say that his arm looked disgusting and that we should pray for him. I was picturing the worst, bone protruding out of his skin. I felt helpless just imagining the pain Marty must have been feeling. Being so far away, on the other side of the world, I could do nothing for him but take Mickele's advice and pray.

This experience gave me a better understanding of Sarah's concerns and worries as she cared for her mother half a world away.

> ## INSPIRATIONAL VERSE
>
> The Lord is good to those whose hope is in
>   him,
> to the one who seeks him;
> it is good to wait quietly
> for the salvation of the Lord.
>
> LAMENTATIONS 3:25–26

MESSAGE

Long-distance caregiving creates a unique set of challenges for both the caregiver and the person or people
being given care. Worry is the dominant emotion I felt
as a long-distance caregiver. When something happens
or changes unexpectedly, the mileage doesn't matter; you
just want to be there as soon as they need you, and it
can be devastating not to be.

I lived literally oceans away from my parents. I was
born and raised in the United Kingdom, but my career
and family took me to Brisbane, Australia. Definitely
not a hop and a skip away! One of my brothers lived a
two-hour drive from our parents, and the other has
lived all over Europe and Asia; so neither was exactly a
stone's throw away either.

My brothers and I staggered our visits so that our
parents always had the "next trip" to look forward to.
This became even more important once they moved
to a residential care home. As age and illness began to
take away many of the freedoms they once enjoyed,

knowing that one of us would arrive on holiday soon kept their focus on being well for our time together. Simply having something to plan for gave them hope, the power of which should never be underestimated.

We would have preferred to keep Mum and Dad in their home, but at that time, professional in-home caregivers were not available in their part of England. My brothers, particularly the one living nearest, had the responsibility of managing our parents' care and finances. They did a fantastic job. But Mum and I had a special and close relationship, and she shared things with me that she probably would not have shared with my brothers. After my father died, Mum needed a higher level of care. She had always feared this and was particularly distressed by the move. Being so far away, I had to rely on feedback from my brothers and made regular calls to her caregivers. The facility was very good and had a stable staff, which helped, but nothing eased my worries until I was able to see her again.

I planned special girl time with Mum during my visits so that we could really reconnect. Mum would always choose to go clothes shopping. We would purchase heaps of clothes and take them back to her room; then over a few days I would help her try them all on and decide which items to keep and which to return. This was less difficult for her than trying to negotiate her walker and, later on, her wheelchair around a changing room. We just had fun going out and doing things she was not able to do on her own or did not wish to do with my brothers. Mum's enthusiasm for our shopping trips was second only to her excitement about going out for a meal at a local pub and simply having a chat.

Mum suffered from Parkinson's. Communication with her became more and more difficult. Her disease quickly took away her ability to write. In the early days when I moved to Australia, we had exchanged letters weekly. When she started to have difficulties with writing, we would call each other alternately on a Sunday evening. This routine was a win-win; it gave Mum something to look forward to each week, and when my father was still alive, it provided him with extra exercise as he paced back and forth reminding us of "how much this phone call is costing me."

Mum's disease eventually affected her hearing and made our weekly calls nearly impossible. I really felt the distance between us once I was no longer able to engage her in a conversation on the telephone. Those calls were our only direct line of communication, and without them, we were lost. The miles were not longer, the oceans were not wider, but Mum was most certainly farther away.

Mum passed over a summer when my brothers were there on holiday. They were with her when she died, which was a great comfort to me. I miss her still, and trips to the UK are not the same without her there, but that constant worry has gone. I have great comfort knowing that her last trip is the one she had always looked forward to the most: reuniting with my father and being cared for eternally.

Sarah Warner

"Simply having something to plan for gave them hope, the power of which should never be underestimated."

CAREGIVER'S PRAYER

God of all Hope and Mercy,

Even though I am living far away from my mother and cannot be with her, I know you can take care of all her needs. I will place my faith and trust in you, O Lord, to prompt me when to call or visit. Please relieve my mother and me of our worries and replace them with peace and calmness. Resting in your promises gives me hope to live one day to the next.

FINDING

GOD'S LESSON

INTRODUCTION

The book *A Man Called Norman* came to mind as I read this next story. The author, Rev. Mike Adkins, humorously describes how his life was changed forever as a result of sharing the Gospel with his misfit neighbor Norman. For years Norman had been ridiculed and judged by the people of their small town because he was a recluse and lived in a run-down house. The Lord began to move on Reverend Mike's heart to care for Norman, wash him, clothe him, love him, and treat Norman like he was family. Mike wrestled with the question "Why me, Lord?—He's so unlovely."

Steve has a similar encounter, with a gentleman by the name of Howie. I love the personal lesson the Lord taught Steve, a life-changing lesson that I will never forget.

INSPIRATIONAL VERSE

"Whatever you did for one of the least of these brothers of mine, you did it for me."

MATTHEW 25:40

MESSAGE

For several years I voluntarily cared for a man named Howie, who was a bit of a hermit, had no family and no running water, and was a hoarder. The social worker assigned to Howie's case warned me that his living conditions were alarming and that several other volunteers had not been able to "make it" after the initial visit. I admit that I gulped when I first saw the shack that Howie called home. It took everything I had to commit myself to care for him. It was a great challenge for me, but where others had failed, I became determined to succeed.

The first months were difficult, but we were able to establish a routine. Once I was able to see past the lack of personal hygiene and the mounds of junk that filled his home, I found that Howie was a great conversationalist and a bit of a charmer. He'd often nudge me as we stood in the checkout line at the local grocery store and say, "Hey, do you see how that clerk is checking me out?" Despite his outward appearance, he had a great smile and made others smile too.

I brought him to my home several times, and he loved my kids. He had a small garden and was sure to give me strawberries and tomatoes to take home to my family. I came to enjoy Howie. I know he appreciated my time and friendship before dementia and Parkinson's disease took control of his mind and body. His home was eventually condemned, and he was forced through legal guardianship to move to a local nursing home.

I continued to visit him regularly for several more years as his health deteriorated. With very poor health habits to begin with, and advancing dementia, he became quite a burden on the facility's staff—often even defecating wherever he pleased. Eventually he couldn't remember my name, became uncommunicative, and mostly lay shaking in his bed.

As I returned home one day after a visit during which I found he had once again made a mess of himself, I asked God why He would allow a person to be such a nuisance to others. Why hadn't God taken Howie, since he wasn't able to speak or think for himself any longer? Then it suddenly occurred to me: Howie was there for me! God was teaching me how to love someone even when he offered nothing in return . . . no conversation, no interaction. What a great lesson for me, and one that gave me strength to continue to care for Howie until his death.

Steve Nooyen

> "*God was teaching me how to love someone even when he offered nothing in return . . . no conversation, no interaction.*"

CAREGIVER'S PRAYER

God of Love,

Your Holy Word tells us to love our neighbors as ourselves. Help me to step out in obedience and follow those instructions. Change my heart, O God, and give me compassion to love others even when they are difficult to love and not able to respond or reciprocate.

ALL THAT GLITTERS
IS NOT GOLD

INTRODUCTION

When I was in grade school, my parents decided to become foster parents for a young redheaded Down syndrome boy named Tommy. He was one year older than I was and had been tossed from one foster home to another. Tommy had typical "boy" experiences while living with us. He broke his arm playing basketball, got a third-degree sunburn on his back because of his fair skin, and got a bloody nose from wrestling with my brothers. But Tommy and my brother Jay did not get along so well. So off Tommy went to another foster home. It was some years later that I saw Tommy at a Catholic church in the neighborhood where my husband, Paul, grew up. I learned that Tommy had been adopted. Finally, after all those years in and out of foster care, he had found a permanent place to call home.

Julie equates finding the best nursing home for

her mother-in-law's needs with finding the right foster home for a child. Julie's frustration and exhaustion come across clearly as she shares her caregiving experience.

INSPIRATIONAL VERSE

I consider that our present sufferings are not worth comparing with the glory that will be revealed in us.

ROMANS 8:18

MESSAGE

Our journey with the elderly began about eight years ago with my sweet mother-in-law, Marjory. Shortly after her husband died, she began to have sleeping problems coupled with anxiety. She had less and less contact with her friends and became reclusive. Marjory was diagnosed with depression and anxiety, and she had inadvertently become addicted to her sleeping pills.

Marjory was placed in a care facility for depressed elderly. We were told at the end of her seven-week stay that she should be moved to assisted living. Marjory was accustomed to a very nice lifestyle, so we chose the facility that we thought would be the most aesthetically pleasing to her.

It did not take long for me to discover that all that glitters is not gold. We encountered tremendous staff turnover and caregivers who were inexperienced with the elderly. So we moved Marjory to a different place to try to find more experienced caretakers. Unfortunately, this was only the first of a number of moves.

Each time we changed facilities, we tried to make Marjory's room as homey as possible. As my mother-in-law got older, she became more comfortable saying what was on her mind. Unfortunately, most of the things on her mind were unpleasant. After we'd worked for hours to make everything perfect, she would walk into her room and say, "I don't like it here." I learned quickly not to take things personally but to try to put myself in her shoes. She wanted to be home instead, but knew she could not be.

Eventually we moved Marjory into a skilled nursing facility because she required physical and occupational therapy. Marjory became delusional and combative within a few short hours. The staff suspected that her dementia was taking a turn for the worse, but an ER doctor diagnosed Marjory with a simple bladder infection. He explained that confusion and frustration are common side effects of any illness with elderly patients but are easily mistaken as signs of dementia. Over time, Marjory became stronger and no longer needed nursing care, so we moved her yet again.

The next place was new and beautiful. Unfortunately, this was a short stay because Marjory pushed her call button too many times. Wanting someone to water her plants was not a good reason to summon help. We were asked to move Marjory out.

This time we decided to try a private home for the elderly with dementia. We were told that this facility had a full-time chef who prepared all the meals. After Marjory had been served hundreds of grilled-cheese sandwiches with bean-and-bacon soup and a side of canned fruit cocktail, I realized this chef had attended a different culinary school than most. Ultimately, in light of other issues, we felt compelled to move Marjory for her own safety.

The owner of the next new facility had a master's degree in nursing, had taken care of her own in-laws, and genuinely loved the elderly. You're probably thinking that we were definitely in the last place for this sweet lady. Wrong! After a little over a year, the owner could no longer afford to keep the home open, and we had a month to find yet another place for Marjory.

By this time, we knew what to look for. The decor of Marjory's next and final home was in need of some TLC, but the staff there was experienced, worked as a team, and genuinely cared for the well-being of their residents. A nurse visited daily, and concerns were addressed immediately and honestly. We had hit the jackpot! Was it perfect? No. But was Marjory well cared for and loved? Yes. To me, that is perfect.

After years of feeling like bad social workers, failing to find a foster child a permanent home, we learned that the real gold is in the heart and not in the decor. Marjory finally found peace. She passed quietly in her sleep several months later, and now she is in the best care ever, the arms of our Savior, Jesus Christ.

Julie Hillmer

"*We had hit the jackpot! Was it perfect? No. But was Marjory well cared for and loved? Yes. To me, that is perfect.*"

CAREGIVER'S PRAYER

Dear Loving God,

Thank you for teaching me so much during these difficult years. Thank you for the perseverance you gave me to make sure that our loved one was well cared for. Father God, show me your glory each day and give me assurance that your grace and guidance are sufficient for us.

LAUGHTER IS A PRECIOUS GIFT

INTRODUCTION

Many of us shortchange ourselves when it comes to realizing our gifts and talents. We all received something of great value from God, and it is our duty and honor to share our gifts and talents with others. Obvious talents such as athletic, artistic, or musical ability; working with your hands; and leading others are often celebrated. We fail to recognize more subtle talents, such as having a joyous spirit, offering the gift of hospitality, or being a great listener. Over the years, I have recognized the gift of encouragement that I have been given. This blessing was not realized right away but was revealed to me over time. Just like Melissa, we may have to do some soul-searching and praying to find out what gifts our Lord has blessed us with.

INSPIRATIONAL VERSE

We have different gifts, according to the grace given us. If a man's gift is prophesying, let him use it in proportion to his faith. If it is serving, let him serve; if it is teaching, let him teach; if it is encouraging, let him encourage; if it is contributing to the needs of others, let him give generously; if it is leadership, let him govern diligently; if it is showing mercy, let him do it cheerfully.

ROMANS 12:6–8

MESSAGE

.I talked to Mom this morning and got the usual guilt trip; no one ever calls, no one ever visits, all of her friends have died. As she continued on and on about how bad everything is, I was thinking that she's right, I don't call or stop in as often as I should. I could stop more often but have chosen not to because she's gotten so grumpy over the years. In my usual fashion, I joked with her: "Well, Ms. Merry Sunshine, maybe if you had nicer things to say, more people would call or visit. C'mon, Mom, less gloom and doom, it's not *that* bad."

She laughed and told me to quit being such a jokester. But that's who I am and it's all that my mom and siblings have come to expect from me. I am not the child who manages her money. I am not the one who does her yard work. She does not ask me to drive her to doctors appointments or to the store. I am the one they ask to bring store-bought dinner rolls and beverages for the holidays. One year they let me make the green bean casserole! But I was never asked again. I am and have always been the class clown, the prankster, and the family entertainment.

After our call today, I felt frustrated with Mom. Why do I even bother? I thought. She never asks about me, my kids, or work. During our call, she mentioned that one of my brothers who lives out of state calls her four times a week. When she said that, I thought: So much for her claim that no one ever calls, . . . and, man, is he a glutton for punishment or what?

She went on to tell me about their new house and what his kids were all doing, that his golf game is getting better. They are going to his wife's family for Christmas this year, but he'll be home for her birthday. He even asks her what the sermon was about on Sundays. Geez, how could I possibly compete with that?

It suddenly hit me. *I wasn't even really listening to her!* And Lord, if you were responsible for that, thank you! I needed it. When Dad died, we all agreed we'd each do our part in caring for Mom, but what had I ever done? Put in my time just enough to stay off the list of people she complained about. What could I do for her anyway? They all had it covered.

It's hard to admit that I have been so selfish. Deep down, I've resented the fact that I was so quickly dismissed from any real responsibility by my siblings. I know I bear the responsibility for that. I've gladly accepted the role of being the one who could always make

Mom laugh but could never really be counted on for anything else.

Had I been listening to her all these years, I would have known that her grumpiness is just to disguise her loneliness. She never was one simply to ask for help when she needed it; she was always the strong and proud matriarch.

The fact is, I haven't done my share in caring for Mom, and it's up to me to change that. I'll work on my relationship with my siblings another day. Today is about Mom. I struggled with how I could start helping after all these years. What could I do for her that wasn't already being done?

Aha! I've got it. I can do what I've always done, make her laugh. How long has it been since I've sat with her and told her the funny stories of my life? How long has it been since I've made her really laugh?

I showed up on Mom's doorstep tonight with a bottle of her favorite wine and asked if she had time to visit. I poured her a glass and didn't ask what she's been up to because I knew the answer to that. Instead I just started telling her stories, and in no time she was laughing. I've missed hearing her laugh; she has a really great laugh.

It may not seem like much, but I asked her if she'd like to make this a weekly date, and she was thrilled to accept. Maybe my role in caring for Mom is to keep her laughing. That's the one thing I know I can do for her.

Melissa Collier

"I struggled with how I could start helping after all these years. What could I do for her that wasn't already being done?"

CAREGIVER'S PRAYER

Giver of Abundant Life,

Thank you for the precious gift of laughter! Please lift the burdens I feel today and let me lift the spirits of those for whom I care. I thank you and praise you, Father, for the unique gifts you have blessed me with and those you have yet to reveal. Continue to use me boldly for your honor and glory.

WISHES COME TRUE

INTRODUCTION

When our daughter Mickele was a freshman in high school, she told us over and over that she was going far away to college. She is definitely our independent child. Her dream was to attend college in New York and perform in Broadway musicals. Yikes! New York? That's so far away and such a big city. I didn't think I would be able to handle the fear of our little girl living in the Big Apple all alone. But after I visited New York with Mickele and saw how she easily maneuvered through the surroundings, God gave me peace about her choice and reminded me to fear not, for He was in control.

Like Mickele, Gary's mother, Trudy, possesses an independent spirit that has led her through life's choices and challenges. As a mother, or as an adult child, it can be hard to let go and allow those we love so dearly to make their own decisions. Gary's story about his mother offered me further peace, showing that God is our navigator and keeps even His most fearless spirits safe.

MESSAGE

The most important lesson that my mother, Trudy, taught my brother, Steven, and me is that none of us has control over what life has in store for us but we do control how we respond to life's surprises. Here is one example that any of us would be lucky to follow.

Mom lost her family in the Holocaust and was left to fend for herself very early in life. This experience taught her to be resilient and tough, but she did not allow it to harden her heart. She immigrated to New York, married, and started a family, only to end up as a divorced mother by the time she was forty-two years old. Certainly not what she had dreamed of, but she refused, once again, to let tragedy define her life. Instead, she became her own fiercely independent person, never asking anyone for anything, loving that she could shape every day of her life from that point on.

Trudy Leiter was by then a true New Yorker. She built a career for herself, but her top priority was always to raise her two sons to be good men, just as tough, resilient, and feisty as their mother. You might not take us for a couple of mama's boys, but there just isn't anything we won't do for our mom. Having been so independent for so long makes it difficult for Mom to accept help, but despite her resistance, we do all we can to make her wishes come true.

Ten years ago she underwent triple bypass surgery and faced a long recovery. Her wish was always to return to the garden apartment where she had lived for the past thirty years, so as quickly as we could, we moved her back to New York. Steven lives in the city and spent every weekend with Mom during her recovery. I saw the caregiving stress in his life. I helped as often as I could, but I never heard a single complaint or negative word from him. For both of us, Mom's happiness and comfort are all that matter. From day one we have been in this together, and I am eternally grateful for that blessing.

Three years ago Mom began to struggle with episodes of congestive heart failure. At that point most people might have considered slowing down, but not Trudy. She had always been an active person, and that wasn't about to change. She fought back and continued to work until she was eighty years old. The truth is that she'd likely still be working had it not been for a car accident that left her unable to drive. That loss of independence was by far the hardest thing for her to accept.

Steven was there for her whenever he was needed, and I kept a bag in my car at all times so I could be there on just a few hours' notice. We also had in-home care for thirty hours each week, but we instructed the caregivers to get Mom out of the apartment. We asked them to take her to her favorite flea markets, to the library (as she always loved to read), out to lunch . . . to do all the things she enjoyed, so she could continue to feel independent. This allowed her to come and go as she pleased without feeling like she had to get our approval or ask for our help.

Hospital admissions became more frequent and hospital stays longer. Mom realized she was too frail to return home from her last hospital admission, so she made the decision to rehabilitate at a long-term care facility. After two months of therapy, she felt like she didn't belong in a nursing home and returned home. Unfortunately, for the first time ever, she was scared of living alone. It wasn't the streets of New York that she was fearful of; it was the walk down her hallway, the trip between her living room and kitchen, climbing into bed at night that made her fear for her own safety. Steven and I saw her feeling like she had just about had enough.

It would have been easy to swoop in and try to take over. But Mom's decisions in life have served her well, and we knew that, beneath her dampened spirits, she was still the same resilient woman she had always been. While it had been her wish to stay in her home, once she knew she wasn't safe, she made the decision to move to assisted living in Rhode Island and has not looked back.

In true Trudy fashion, she is embracing her new life just as she chose to do so many years ago. She could have held on to a home that no longer met her needs and continued to decline. Instead, she continues to shape her life by responding positively to a new home and a new definition of independence. Her life lessons now serve as an example to her grandchildren. Not a day goes by without my thanking God for the glory of being her son.

Mom now lives five minutes away from me, and Steven is the one who keeps a bag packed. We have both found peace because Mom is in the best place for her and is getting stronger rather than declining. Most important, she is being cared for and wants to live longer because she is happy! That is definitely a wish that Steven and I will go to any lengths to see come true.

Gary Leiter

"She could have held on to a home that no longer met her needs and continued to decline. Instead, she continues to shape her life by responding positively to a new home and a new definition of independence."

CAREGIVER'S PRAYER

Sovereign God,

You are in control of all things. Help me to reassure my loved ones that they are safe in their environment and that you are watching over them day and night. You are the true source of security when I am confronted by worldly fears. Give me peace so I may rest secure in your promise.

SHOWER ME WITH LOVE

INTRODUCTION

There is a certain intimacy between a mother and daughter, a bond in which truth and honesty begin. I remember it was my junior year in high school when I started to tell my mother the truth about everything. I mean everything! Some were things she probably didn't want to hear and were perhaps even a little uncomfortable, but she was there for me. I was able to trust and confide in her, which has allowed the two of us to share an intimate relationship to this day. I pray that my three daughters and I share this same trusted bond. Jeanne and her mother shared a special closeness that carried them through some difficult and awkward moments.

INSPIRATIONAL VERSE

For you created my inmost being;
you knit me together in my mother's womb.
I praise you because I am fearfully and wonderfully made.

PSALM 139:13–14

MESSAGE

I have many fond memories of caring for my mother before she died. When Mom was diagnosed with terminal cancer, we moved her and Dad into our home to care for them. I had prepared myself for it to be a difficult time but was unexpectedly surprised that those final months with Mom were quite extraordinary. It was heartbreaking to be losing her, but the time we shared during the last chapter of her life has given me some of my most treasured memories of her.

One of my favorite memories will always be the first time I helped her bathe. Mom was always a very modest person, so it meant a lot to me when she asked me to help her take a shower. She knew she was too weak to do it by herself, but I was concerned about whether she would be comfortable with my help.

Luckily our shower had a built-in seat, which made things easier. Mom was able to sit while I washed her back and her hair. I was there to help her stand when she was able, so she felt safe. I talked to her about the things we would normally talk about over a cup of coffee to keep her mind off any awkwardness she may have felt.

After I helped her dry off, I put some fragrant body lotion on her. We giggled about how good she smelled "just to go to bed," and how a simple shower can make you feel so good. I could tell by the look on her face that she truly appreciated our time together that evening. I did too.

Privacy is a difficult thing to maintain while battling an illness, so in many ways, conquering that first shower brought us closer together. It made us stronger to get past the hurdles Mom faced as she needed more and more help. There is a special intimacy that happens when you are caring for someone during her most private and vulnerable moments. Mom and I had always been close, but it was there, in her inner sanctum, that we formed a bond that will always belong to just the two of us.

I thank God that He gave me those special memories to cherish. Mom has been gone for three years now, but I will never forget how I was able to give back to her for the wonderful things she had done for me.

Jeanne Griffith

"*There is a special intimacy that happens when you are caring for someone during her most private and vulnerable moments.*"

CAREGIVER'S PRAYER

Creator God,

How majestic is your name in all the earth. Thank you for our blessed mothers, who took care of us from birth. May I do the best I can to care for my mother now in her times of need in the delicate ways that bring her joy. Let her know how much I love her by my gentle touch and through my encouraging words. May our moments together be meaningful.

A FAMILY RESPONSIBILITY

INTRODUCTION

Our whole family helped raise my younger brother, Jay, who was mentally handicapped. I say "was" because he passed away in 2001 of a seizure at age thirty-seven. There were many trying times and situations as we were growing up. Jay had dramatic mood swings because he was bipolar, which resulted in physically aggressive behavior followed by bouts of depression and excessive dependence. I remember the times when my mother had bruises from the mini-wars waged while getting Jay ready for school.

As I look back on those years, I realize the gifts brought forth from those experiences, for which I am forever grateful. My brother helped to shape my character. I learned to be a more loving, patient adult and to have a greater understanding and compassion for those with special needs. Even the apostle Paul encourages us to rejoice in our sufferings, because we know that suffering produces perseverance; perseverance, character; and character, hope (Romans 5:3). I believe where there is hope, there is love. And Jay was loved dearly by our family and others who knew him.

Kay perseveres through some trying times with her handicapped son, Pat. God shows us on a daily basis how His love and strength sustain us from one moment to the next.

INSPIRATIONAL VERSE

He gives strength to the weary
    and increases the power of the weak.
Even youths grow tired and weary,
and young men stumble and fall;
but those who hope in the Lord
will renew their strength.
They will soar on wings like eagles;
they will run and not grow weary,
they will walk and not be faint.

ISAIAH 40:29–31

MESSAGE

This is simply my life. I am not a hero. I do not feel extraordinary or special. I do what all mothers do: care for the needs of my children. One of them happens to have special needs. For that I feel blessed and grateful, but it hasn't always been that way.

Complications at the end of my first pregnancy caused our son, Pat, to arrive four weeks early. Although there are always concerns with a premature birth, the doctors were actually far more worried about me than about the baby. The delivery went well, and we were thrilled to welcome our new son into our lives.

Pat developed normally for the first three to four months, but when he was six months old, he began having seizures. I was terrified and overwhelmed as the doctors stabilized his condition and began further testing. During the next several months, people would often remind me that God gives us only what we can handle, but I didn't necessarily agree with that statement at the time.

I am a woman of deep faith, but when faced with this challenge as a young woman and wife, I often questioned God, "Can I do this?" But God was with me as I made it through ten minutes, then thirty minutes, half a day, a full day, and one week, and I knew He had always been my source of strength. Armed with God's love, I felt ready to handle whatever challenges lay ahead.

There is no way to prepare yourself to learn that your one-year-old son has been diagnosed with developmental disabilities. And there was no way to predict the worst of it when his diagnosis became multiple disabilities and genetic disorders, such as cerebral palsy, severe and profound deficiencies, and uncontrolled seizures.

I guess God does give us what we can handle, because He blessed my husband, Mark, and me with two more wonderful sons, Dayne and Brad. They grew up understanding that Pat has special needs. We've always said that this was a family responsibility. They helped to care for Pat with strength and grace.

Pat functions at the level of an infant and requires complete care, so the entire family is involved with dressing, feeding, giving meds, and changing his diapers. He can sit up independently, roll around, and grab things with his right hand, so he cannot be left unattended. Much like an infant, he doesn't know if he is near something that can hurt him or if he's grabbing something he shouldn't. Pat communicates with us nonverbally, through facial expressions. He smiles, laughs, and gives us, as his brother calls it, the "hairy eye" when he isn't happy with something.

I travel for my job, and my husband works outside the home, so Dayne and Brad help care for their brother. I had always assumed this was the case with most families like ours until I attended a Mother's Day brunch for women with severe and profound special needs children. I commented on how involved my other sons were with their brother. One woman said: "My daughters would never do anything to help their brother." Many of the other mothers nodded in agreement. I remember feeling shocked but also exceptionally blessed to have the kind of family that cares so much.

Dayne and Brad are grown now; they're building their lives and may soon begin families of their own. I could not be more proud of the men they have become. My husband and I can't wait to see what they will do with their lives. They will remain involved with Pat. However, when I stop to think about how life will undoubtedly change as they follow the natural course of their lives, I am overcome with emotions: excitement for them, but a sense of sadness too. Knowing that Pat's life will never change and that ours will be defined by our choice to care for him can cause a wave of tears and a feeling of being overwhelmed.

I wouldn't change a thing, even if I could. We've embraced the hand we were dealt and are a closer family because of it. However, the reality is that at a time when most couples are preparing to be empty nesters, we may have less freedom and less time together as a couple.

It really hits me sometimes how different our lives are relative to the lives of our peers. It's not pity I feel but rather a deep appreciation of God's love. I know that our special circumstance with Pat has had an impact on our extended family and friends. Not everything is as easy or convenient as it might have been otherwise. But it has never mattered; God has taken special care to surround us with people who accept us just as we are, not as a special needs child or a special needs family. We are just a family using our God-given talents to do the best we can each and every day, like everyone else does.

Kay Shields

"But God was with me as I made it through ten minutes, then thirty minutes, half a day, a full day, and one week, and I knew He had always been my source of strength."

CAREGIVER'S PRAYER

O Gracious Lord,

You are my strength every morning and my salvation in times of distress. Thank you for giving me what I need from one moment to the next. Even when I feel powerless, you are powerful and provide a resource of strength that can come only from you, Lord. When trials come my way, I know that you are always with me.

THAT'S JUST PEACHY

INTRODUCTION

Knowing that a loved one is destined for heaven is a true comfort and joy. My brother Jay was mentally handicapped and loved the Lord. When he passed away, there was no doubt in my mind that he was in heaven. I knew he was with Jesus because of his childlike faith, and I had confirmation just days after his funeral while I was walking through Kmart, of all places. It was as if a beam of light were shining down on a jigsaw puzzle at the end of the aisle. It had a picture of Jesus in heaven, hugging a brown-haired, slightly balding young man. I knew in my heart that God was telling me that my brother Jay was with Him now in paradise.

Becky and her grandfather, peachy, make quite the pair as she helps him find that same paradise.

INSPIRATIONAL VERSE

For God did not appoint us to suffer wrath but to receive salvation through our Lord Jesus Christ. He died for us so that, whether we are awake or asleep, we may live together with him. Therefore encourage one another and build each other up, just as in fact you are doing.

I THESSALONIANS 5:9–11

MESSAGE

The day before I left for a college graduation trip to England, my paternal grandfather, whom I lovingly called Peachy, had emergency open-heart surgery. Peachy had a hard exterior, but he always had a soft spot for me. We shared a special bond. I was there during the surgery but had to leave the next day before he was out of the woods. I called home throughout the trip, and my mother would tell me everything was fine, but I knew she was sugar-coating something. Peachy had suffered a massive stroke.

When I saw Peachy for the first time after the stroke, he was totally unresponsive. I talked to him and told him all about the trip—still nothing. But on that visit, before I left, I went to kiss him, and although he was unable to move his right side, the left side of his lips puckered to kiss me back. And so the journey that families go through in these situations began for us. After rehabilitation was over, decisions about Peachy's care needed to be made.

Since I was right out of college and the most available, I offered to live with him. My family appreciated my
gusto, but it immediately became apparent that Peachy's
needs were more than I could handle alone. Arrangements were made for in-home care Monday through
Friday, and our family took different shifts at night and
on the weekends. Peachy had been divorced for many
years from my grandmother, whom we called Darlin',
so he was used to being on his own and was a little set
in his ways.

My mother was a Christian, and my sister and I
were raised in the house of the Lord. Peachy had not
been religious. By the time I was six, I knew what it
meant *not* to be a Christian, and it became my goal to
do whatever it took to get Peachy to the Lord. I prayed
incessantly for his salvation.

I was an anxious little girl to begin with, so as you
can imagine, worrying about the salvation of one of the
most important men in my life caused me a lot of turmoil. Through Scripture, God found His way to calm my
heart: *Be anxious for nothing* (Phil 4:6). As if to say, *Becky,
I've got this one; don't worry.* God let me know that it wasn't
my job to offer salvation; it was His.

Peachy began to change. I think having our family
there caring for him made him realize for the first time
the depth of our love. Through the pain, he had begun
to soften, and he was more open than he had ever been.
Although communication was difficult for him after
the stroke, he talked and laughed more than he had in
years.

One of the funniest moments happened when I asked Peachy to go with Dad and me to look at a car I wanted to buy. Along the way, we stopped into Wendy's for a quick bite. Dad took Peachy to the restroom while I ordered. It was taking them quite a while, so I went to check on them. I knocked, and Dad opened the door for me to see him and Peachy standing with water covering the fronts of both their shirts, their hands, and their faces. I'm not sure what had happened, but the three of us couldn't stop laughing about how "handicapped-accessible" isn't necessarily the same thing as being handicapped-friendly.

I had the Saturday-evening shift the week Peachy passed. When I came on shift that night, I heard noises coming from his room. It was very difficult for Peachy to move on his own, so I was surprised to see that he was sitting up on the side of his bed. He called me over to talk, but I was way too tired to listen and told him that we should just catch up in the morning. Not talking to him on that night will forever be my biggest regret.

The next morning, my mom came to relieve me so that I could go to church. I invited Peachy to come along, but he declined. By the time I reached the church, my mom called with the glorious news that Peachy had changed his mind and that I should meet them out front. I will never forget how it felt to walk into church with him on that Sunday. The congregation was singing "Amazing Grace," and even though he couldn't talk very well, under his breath Peachy was trying to sing along.

The following Thursday, we received a call from the caregiver saying that he had found Peachy on the floor and thought maybe it was a heart attack. We were there in time to perform CPR. I was asked to continue chest compressions even after EMS arrived, and I remember looking down at Peachy, knowing he was dying despite our attempts to save him.

I prayed to the Lord and begged Him, "If Peachy doesn't know you yet, Lord, please just give him one more chance. And if he does know you, Lord, please give me a sign that he's with you." It was in that moment that I felt as if I was simply melting over Peachy. All my years of anxiousness were instantly replaced with absolute peace, knowing that as much as I loved Peachy, Jesus Christ had him in His hands now and that He loved him even more than I did.

Becky Beanblossom

"*Worrying about the salvation of one of the most important men in my life caused me a lot of turmoil. . . . God let me know that it wasn't my job to offer salvation; it was His.*"

CAREGIVER'S PRAYER

Amazing Jesus,

Let me have childlike faith, pure and innocent. The strong faith that sets me free from worry and doubt also offers me comfort and joy. Help me to continually put my faith and trust in you, O Lord, for your ways are perfect.

TWO COUNTRIES, TWO HOMES

INTRODUCTION

One of my mentors once shared a message with me that I found very thought-provoking. It has helped me focus on what is important in life and not get caught up in the world's view of "success." He told me that we are not called to be successful; we are called to be faithful—faithful to God, faithful to our spouse, faithful to our family, faithful to our career, and faithful to our friends. When we are faithful, then we are successful.

Faithful devotion to her family, despite feelings of guilt and regret, has encouraged Yoshino to change the face of aging all around the world, starting with her own parents in Japan.

INSPIRATIONAL VERSE

I thank Christ Jesus our Lord, who has given me strength, that he considered me faithful, appointing me to his service.

I TIMOTHY 1:12

MESSAGE

As soon as I learned there was a place called America, I knew I wanted to go there. At that point, the only thing I really knew about America was that it is the country where you can become anything you dream of if you work hard enough. God bless my parents, who looked beyond their beliefs and traditions to support my dreams, even if that meant I would move across the world to achieve those dreams.

I entered the American Field Service Exchange Program and came to study in America during my senior year of high school. The plan was for me to go back to Japan for college, but during my time in America, I applied to and was accepted at the University of Minnesota. My life as a long-distance daughter and sister had officially begun. From that point forward, I would have two families and two countries to consider home.

Business came naturally to me, and I built a successful career in franchising. One of those businesses asked that I expand their franchises to Poland, where I lived for a short time, with the intent of moving back to the States as soon as I could. While in Poland, of all places,

I learned about Paul Hogan, who gave me the opportunity to become the global development officer for Home Instead Senior Care.

It is said that God works in mysterious ways. From a professional perspective, this was an opportunity that exceeded even the wildest dreams of that little Japanese girl who still lives inside my heart. Personally, this "job" meant something different. I have always carried a heavy amount of guilt over not being in Japan to help care for my parents as they aged. I began to wonder: Could making in-home senior care an option in my homeland help ease my guilt for not being a caregiver to my own parents?

I have two brothers and a sister who live in Japan, but I still felt guilt about not doing my part or carrying my share of the responsibility. Japanese tradition dictates that seniors are cared for by family and is resistant to bringing outsiders into the home. I knew that accepting in-home caregiving would be a gradual process that would begin with an invitation to green tea in the front garden only before being invited farther into the home. But I also knew that my parents, siblings, and millions of others like them could benefit from its support. It was that belief that inspired me to make Japan among our first global territories at Home Instead Senior Care.

Despite my role in global senior care, it wasn't until my parents needed more care that I truly began to appreciate the impact that age, illness, and care decisions have on the entire family. Although I've traveled the world advocating for advancement in senior care, nothing has been more rewarding than to fulfill my responsibility as a daughter and a sister. No amount of professional accomplishment could erase the guilt I felt. Nor could it replace the immense satisfaction of knowing that my parents were receiving the care they needed even though I was six thousand miles away. To me, caregiving is a universal tradition that should never be broken.

Yoshino Nakajima

> *"Although I've traveled the world advocating for advancement in senior care, nothing has been more rewarding than to fulfill my responsibility as a daughter and a sister."*

CAREGIVER'S PRAYER

Faithful and Loving Father,

Help me always to put you first in my life. Your Word tells us that when we honor you, you honor us in return. Please wash away my guilt for not doing enough for my parents because of the distance that separates us. And replace my guilt with confidence and strength in knowing that I will be given the crown of life for my faithful devotion unto you.

WHEN DREAMS FADE

INTRODUCTION

My parents, Jan and Larry, kept my grandpa Damrow very young at heart by taking him on cross-country trips from Maine to California in their RV. Even the dog and cat managed to tag along for some furry companionship. To celebrate his ninety-seventh birthday, all of our families went camping together at Mahoney State Park in Nebraska. We roasted hot dogs and marshmallows on the open fire and told stories until the last ember faded. We all cherished that special time with Grandpa and remarked that we wanted still to be camping at age ninety-seven just like he had done. This must be one of the secrets to successful aging—keeping one's self active, challenging mind, body, and spirit while trying something new and different. Grandpa taught us by his example to live every day to the fullest.

God has a sovereign plan for each of us, but oftentimes that plan is disguised in challenges. James learned through his caregiving experience that the more challenging a situation, the more impact it has on our life.

INSPIRATIONAL VERSE

In his heart a man plans his course,
but the Lord determines his steps.

PROVERBS 16:9

MESSAGE

It had been my father's dream to retire and travel across the country in his motor home. He always loved the outdoors. Retirement was supposed to be an exciting time for him and my mother to go to the places they had always wanted to see, to enjoy a new chapter of life together. Shortly after his retirement and their first trips, however, I began to notice subtle changes in my father's behavior and memory. It quickly became apparent that I could see the early signs of Alzheimer's but that my mother could not. Or would not.

For a couple of years my parents continued to take short trips. Still wanting to make my father's retirement dreams come true, my mother decided she would do the driving. But after a few short trips, she realized that she could not continue to do so. She sold the motor home as acceptance that retirement would not be the adventure they had dreamed it would be.

My father was diagnosed with both Alzheimer's and Parkinson's, which had progressed to the point that Mom could not handle him by herself. I tried to convince Mom that she needed help. But being a product of her generation, she said to me, "In sickness and in health, till death do us part, I can take care of him."

My sister and I agreed that Mom would benefit from additional help. A church member introduced me to a professional caregiver. In order for Mom to agree to meet her, I had to "back-door" my way in by telling my mother that this woman really needed employment. After that meeting, Mom admitted that she could use some help, and the caregiver started working three days a week. Mom came to appreciate her help.

This first caregiver was able to help for almost a year before Dad needed further care. Luckily, another church member told me about someone who had been doing this kind of work all her life. She started immediately, working from Sunday evening after her church service through Friday evening after Dad was in bed. The responsibility then shifted back to me, my sister, friends, and family.

This caregiver worked with Dad for fifteen months before she said she just could not do it any longer. I had been talking with my mom about getting Dad's name on the waiting list at a nursing home, but she would not agree to that. But her sister-in-law and her neighbor convinced my mom to visit some nursing homes. Dad was placed in the Hamilton County Nursing Home and two weeks later he developed pneumonia and had to be transported to Memorial Hospital. He passed away five days later, the day before his seventy-third birthday.

Before his death, my wife, Sandra, and I had been praying over the decision to start our own business. Three months after my dad's death I found the opportunity to serve seniors. Was this part of God's sovereign plan? My background as a hospital accountant and

Sandra being an RN made it apparent that perhaps this was what we were called to do.

Over time my mother's health began to worsen. She had become close with a church friend who had also recently lost her husband. Together they were able to take trips that they would have loved to be taking with their husbands. Mom enjoyed staying in the time-share that had been Dad's favorite spot to visit. But after one trip, Mom confided in Sandra that she did not have any energy. She was admitted to the hospital for testing. She showed signs of pre-leukemia, and less than four months later, two days before Thanksgiving, Mom passed away.

I felt like we were able to provide Mom with the right care and comfort during her last months and weeks. Not only were we there but Hospice of Chattanooga also cared for her. It was a real asset to have A+ caregivers help us keep Mom in her home and give her the care she deserved. I only wish we had been able to do the same for Dad.

It has been fourteen years since Sandra and I started our business providing seniors with in-home care and companionship. To use the knowledge learned through the very different experiences of my own parents' deaths to help others is a blessing. We asked God for guidance about a new business, and He answered our prayer. He provided us with an honor greater than we could ever have wished for: to serve families in very similar situations. God rewards us abundantly each and every day.

James Gardenhire

"I felt like we were able to provide Mom with the right care and comfort during her last months and weeks."

CAREGIVER'S PRAYER

Most High God,

The road traveled in life can become so weary and worn. Thank you, Lord, for going before us every step of the way as we seek your revelation while making care decisions for our senior loved ones. You do immeasurably more than all we ask or imagine, and you know what we need before we even ask. You are faithful to provide when we put our trust in you.

EASY GIVING!

INTRODUCTION

When Paul and I started Home Instead Senior Care in 1994, we enlisted the help of several family members. My mother, Jan, was our first office assistant as well as a part-time caregiver. She had a natural love for seniors and enjoyed spending time with our elderly clients. We matched her with a former senator who needed a caregiver to cook for him and his adult son. Mom would cook up a storm on Tuesdays, preparing meals to put in the freezer for the entire week. His favorite recipes lacked flavor or variety, so she slowly introduced her own delicious recipes. Soon they were hooked on her nutritious dishes and fresh-baked pies. Mom was a huge hit with the senator and his son. When they praised her cooking, it made her feel needed and rewarded.

Mom found that one of the most satisfying aspects of caregiving is the feeling of being there to help someone who truly needs care. She found joy as a daughter and caregiver for her father and extended that joy to others.

INSPIRATIONAL VERSE

"Give, and it will be given to you. A good measure, pressed down, shaken together and running over, will be poured into your lap. For with the measure you use, it will be measured to you."

LUKE 6:38

MESSAGE

I didn't realize until after my dad died how much I missed being his caregiver. Of course, a great deal of that feeling was because I missed him. Even though my caregiving phase was short, it was special to me. After all, he and Mom had been my caregivers, not only when I was a dependent child but off and on throughout my life. So it was just a matter of returning the favor, and I felt good about it.

My folks took good care of themselves well into their eighties. They sold their home and moved into a nice assisted living community. Dad was a good planner, and fortunately, he had all their legal and financial matters taken care of. But after Mom died, things changed. Dad became increasingly feeble and was using a walker. Several times I got calls in middle of the night informing me that he had been taken to the hospital. That meant a ninety-mile drive from Omaha to Beatrice to look in on him. We decided it would be better if he could move closer.

The hard part was trying to persuade him to leave

his hometown, where he had lived his entire life, and move to Omaha. Together, we found a very nice assisted living center that was near our home. When Dad moved to Omaha, he seemed to perk up. He no longer used his walker, and he would participate in all the activities at his new home. Dad may have missed his hometown, friends, and church, but I was proud of how quickly he became part of the community at his residence.

There wasn't much caregiving to do, except small chores like his laundry. He was well cared for, and we felt fortunate to have found a place that truly assisted its residents. I wished for a more active role in Dad's actual care, but he needed medical attention that I could not provide. Caregiving takes many different forms and sometimes inches in on your life rather than taking it over. Dad's simple caregiving needs eased into my life, and I accepted what I could and could not do for him.

Dad was with us every weekend so we could all go to church together and have Sunday dinner at our home, which he loved. The grandchildren and great-grandchildren were a blessing to him. We even took him in our new motor home on a two-week vacation to the Northeast. At the age of ninety-five, he still proved he could be a "trooper."

After he died, I felt envious of friends who still were caring for a parent. I didn't have the chance to have Dad stay with us as was planned when, and if, he got out of the hospital. I wasn't given the chance to care for my father for as long as I had wanted, but I was inspired by the many people who played a role in his care over the years. I believe that if you have care to give, you should give it. It always comes back to you in immeasurable doses.

Jan Novicki

> "*Caregiving takes many different forms and sometimes inches in on your life rather than taking it over.*"

CAREGIVER'S PRAYER

You alone are the Lord, blessed be your glorious name,

You give me great joy and satisfaction from serving my parent and other seniors. I feel as though caregiving is a gift from you that I am grateful to receive. Every good and perfect gift comes from above. Allow me to continue to bless others and care for their needs as you place these desires upon my heart.

THE CARING
DOESN'T END

INTRODUCTION

Recently, my father and I were having that "awkward" conversation. No, not the "birds and the bees"! The "aging" conversation. Where do you want to age? Do you have a will? Who has your power of attorney? Have you written end-of-life directives? I figured my parents and I should have this conversation since they are in their early seventies, and they still have their faculties and can make solid decisions as to how they want to age. Too often people wait until there is a crisis situation, and then it is too late.

My father told me exactly where my parents' important papers were kept. He also told me that they have funeral plots and arrangements already made, including Scripture verses, music, program, and time of funeral—seven o'clock in the evening so no one would have to get off work. I was so relieved he did not tell me the date! That would have been freaky! I was grateful for this conversation and felt as though it was a blessing to us kids. It also gave me a better understanding of my parents' wishes so that I can help them accordingly as they age.

Danielle's story is a cautionary tale. She candidly shares her regret about not taking the time to discuss end-of-life directives with her parents before it was too late.

INSPIRATIONAL VERSE

I lift my eyes to the hills—
where does my help come from?
My help comes from the Lord,
the Maker of heaven and earth.

PSALM 121:1–2

MESSAGE

Each night when I pull into my driveway, I open the garage door and stare at the boxes of my mother's belongings, which serve as a painful reminder of my recent loss. It is in these moments each day that I feel as if I am on a deserted island. At thirty-one years old, I am an only child who has lost both parents. I have a strong support system, but sometimes it feels like I've been left to fend for myself.

Dad died of a massive heart attack when I was twenty. While his death was devastating, Mom and I had each other and became closer than ever as we grieved together. Their wills and his affairs were in order, which made the business end of his death much easier to deal with than it would have been otherwise. We missed him terribly, but slowly, we moved forward with our lives, as he would have wanted.

Mom passed only a few months ago, so the pain of her death is still raw and tender. In contrast to the sudden death of my dad, I was not prepared for the tasks at hand when Mom was diagnosed with Stage IV ovarian cancer. It was a two-year battle with ups and downs of remission, chemotherapy, and hospice.

Caring for her during those two years was an honor but also a real eye-opener for me. I discovered that I was stronger than I thought I could be, especially when it came to things such as helping with her feeding tube and going with her to chemotherapy. Still, it was a lot to handle, and although I found the strength to be with her every step of the way, I'd be lying if I said it was easy.

Her motherly instinct to protect me never wavered, even during Mom's darkest days. It was frustrating that she didn't always communicate with me openly about her condition. I felt bad that I didn't know everything I needed to know. Part of that was her denial, and the other part was that we were so close. I really had that amazing lady fooled into believing I was the perfect child, and I know she didn't want to burden me. She didn't want me to miss work or miss time with my friends and would often say, "Danielle, go live your life!"

That time together provided us opportunity to do a lot of living, talking, and laughing. In many ways, it was as though God gave us a chance to say good-bye, something neither of us had with Dad. Only you can't prepare yourself for the loss of someone so deeply loved. You can try, you can tell yourself it's for the best if they don't suffer long and you can pray to God, but in the end, the death itself is not any easier for those left behind. I was by Mom's side, my head on her lap, when she passed. It was so peaceful and I felt relief that she didn't linger, but the pain of the loss was not lessened.

While Mom was sick, there were times I selfishly wanted to be alone with her and felt irritated when others took her time away from me. I had to realize that she had not just been my mother. She was also a sister, friend, and daughter. After her death, the people to whom she had been all those things were there for me, but I didn't really know how anyone could help. Only after a few months and the first holidays without her did I crash and burn. I sought professional help, and grief counseling is slowly helping me heal.

In the meantime, the caring doesn't end. Now I am caring for Mom by handling her affairs, getting things "settled." Despite all the conversations we had, we never discussed her will, life insurance, et cetera. I am her sole heir, but she never changed the name of her beneficiary after Dad died, which has complicated matters. Being asked to produce death certificates as proof to insurance companies has been unspeakably difficult. I kick myself every day for not asking the tough questions and making sure everything was in order before her death. Significant changes, like the death of a spouse or parent, require changes to wills and insurance policies. However difficult it may be, I urge everyone to save

yourself the heartache and have those discussions before it is too late.

Because we had not, I was left to scour Mom's files
and laptop, hoping to find a Dear Danielle letter to give
me some guidance. I didn't find exactly what I hoped
for, but she did leave a list of where her current research
files should be delivered. Mom had been a renowned
certified oral myologist and speech pathologist, and she
wrote a book to help children who sucked their thumbs
and fingers. As I sorted through her office, I saw how
many lives she had touched through her work, and I
was overcome with pride. I plan to go on caring for her
legacy by starting a scholarship in her name, Rose Van
Norman, to enable others to continue her research.

Which takes me back to the garage full of her
things . . . Through counseling, I've learned to take
things slowly and grieve at my own pace. I need to
go through the boxes and decide what to keep and
what to give away, but I'm just not ready for that yet. I
know her spirit transcends the material possessions sitting in my garage, but for now, having her things
nearby comforts me.

It would be easy to question God's motives and be
angry, but somehow I have found peace. My parents
may not be here in body, but their spirits are being well
cared for within my heart. Yes, I miss them. There
will be a bittersweetness as the events of my life unfold.
I'll want my father to walk me down the aisle someday,
and I'll want to have my mother by my side when I have
children. And it will always be their advice that I long

for. But they instilled in me good values, common sense, and a deep faith that I am relying on as I find my way. This certainly isn't the outcome I would have ever wished for, but no matter what life has in store for me next, I have two angels cheering me on from the best seats in the house.

Danielle Van Norman

"I kick myself every day for not asking the tough questions and making sure everything was in order before her death."

CAREGIVER'S PRAYER

Lord, you are the God of Details,

Please give me the wisdom and sense of timing to talk to my parents about their desired future care. What a blessing to know how they want to age. Enable me to follow their plan, Lord. Help me to gather my important papers and affairs together for my children, so that they can have peace of mind knowing that my wishes are recorded.

I HAVE MY OWN LIFE

INTRODUCTION

Caregiving can be very demanding of a person's time and energy. It's a balancing act between work-related responsibilities, household chores, and caring for a family member. It's like burning a candle at both ends and the wick is getting shorter and shorter. Resentment and frustration often result because siblings have not offered to help and the brunt of the care rests on the shoulders of one.

Before your wick burns out and you sit smoldering, read how this daughter faced these same common circumstances and found a solution to restore balance in her life.

INSPIRATIONAL VERSE

"Come to me, all you who are weary and burdened, and I will give you rest. Take my yoke upon you and learn from me, for I am gentle

> and humble in heart, and you will find rest
> for your souls. For my yoke is easy and my
> burden is light."
>
> MATTHEW 11:28–30

MESSAGE

It's important for you to know that there are four of us—two brothers and two sisters. My dad is gone, so it's just Mom, and she's at a point now of needing support more frequently. Although she is active, continues to work, and lives on her own, I am starting to worry about her future care.

As the oldest daughter, I'm the one she calls—for everything. If she has doctors appointments or problems in her apartment, when she's sick or lonely, I'm the one she counts on first. My husband and I have shouldered the bulk of her care, through no fault of hers or my siblings' but rather out of convenience and the duty of being the eldest child.

Most of the time, it's fine. I love my mom and can manage the additional responsibilities. But there are those days when I just feel angry at her for not considering my life. Mom forgets that I have a full-time job and a family of my own. It's not uncommon for her to schedule a medical appointment before checking if I am available. It's as though she doesn't understand that I may be traveling or have an important business meeting at that time. Somehow, in her mind, I'm always available, or should be.

It can also be easy to resent my brothers and sisters for not stepping in to help more often. In all fairness, they are there when I ask, but why should I even have to ask them to help? She's their mom too. There was a time not long ago that my brother (Bill), who lives out of state, offered to drive in and take her to the doctor. I was so happy that he was trying to help, but she told him she couldn't possibly ask him to make that trip when she could get me to do it instead. I resented that Mom somehow felt she couldn't impose on Bill but could so easily impose on me.

That was when I knew I needed to make some changes but wasn't sure how. My boss had been in a similar situation, so I asked what she would suggest I do. She told me that it wouldn't be easy but that I needed to set boundaries and be willing to enforce those boundaries by telling Mom, "I'm sorry, I'm not available. You'll have to make other arrangements." That suggestion was genius, and I kicked myself for not thinking of it myself!

My boss's simple advice reminded me of days when my children were growing up. Every phase of their lives required a learning curve, and sometimes it took a bit of "tough love," but it always came down to boundaries. Mom would often tell me, especially when my children were teenagers, that they were "just testing my limits." I think, without realizing it, she was doing the same to me now.

Somehow, it was far easier to say no to my children than to my mother, but it seems to be working. I calmly and gently explained how caregiving is a family opportunity and that my sister and brothers are available and ready to help. There was something liberating about admitting, to Mom and to myself, that I simply cannot always be there for her and that we both need my brothers' and sister's involvement. My boss was right, it wasn't easy, but being open and honest feels much better than being angry and resentful.

Anonymous

{ *"Somehow, in her mind, I'm always available, or should be."* }

CAREGIVER'S PRAYER
God of Peace,

I thank you that I can come to you when my burdens get heavy. Take away my anger and resentment and let me take up your yoke. Show me how to set boundaries lovingly with my family. And please humble me to recognize those times when I need help from my siblings, friends, or a professional caregiver.

HEART AND SOUL

INTRODUCTION

As young girls, my sister Wendy and I couldn't wait to visit my grandparents for a week in the summer. We knew they would prepare all our favorite desserts and play all our favorite card games. They enjoyed entertaining, and their social calendar was filled with luncheons, bridge parties, church meetings, and Lions Club dinners. Food was definitely the focal point for all their gatherings. My grandparents were fortunate to lead independent, social lives that kept them actively engaged with friends and their community.

I wouldn't call my grandparents "party animals," but Martin Warner lovingly describes his mother as a "party animal" in the story you are about to read.

....

INSPIRATIONAL VERSE

"You are the light of the world. A city on a hill cannot be hidden. Neither do people light

> a lamp and put it under a bowl. Instead they put it on its stand, and it gives light to everyone in the house. In the same way, let your light shine before men, that they may see your good deeds and praise your Father in heaven."
>
> MATTHEW 5:14–16

MESSAGE

Back in the day, my mother may have been considered a party animal. She was highly social, up for anything, and she loved to entertain. She gave my brothers and me the lifelong gift of an amazing childhood in London, and then adulthood in the Queensland state of Australia. I know we were well cared for, but my memories are full of how fun it was having her as a mom.

Mom's health and mobility have slowly declined because of spina bifida. Dad had been her primary caregiver, only to be diagnosed with terminal lung cancer himself. As she grieved the loss of my father, Mom also grieved her perceived loss of freedom.

In a short period of time, I had become a roundabout husband of sorts, filling Dad's shoes as Mom's primary caregiver. She lived ten minutes away from us, but her limited mobility made living alone too difficult to manage. Mom was angry over the loss of her independence and took that frustration out on me and my wife, Sarah. We told her that she didn't need to do that; our love and care for her is unconditional. I assured her that there are options and choices in every situation and that we would find the best solution for her.

My mother's spirit is the exact same as it has always been. Only now, that party animal is trapped inside a body that cannot do what she so desperately wants it to do. It isn't always easy dealing with her frustration, but I can certainly understand it and empathize with her. We had to find a solution that allowed her to live on her own while also getting the help and care she needed.

Fortunately, on the land where our home sits, there was room to build a granny shack (perhaps known elsewhere as a guesthouse). Mom would never have agreed to living in our home with us, so moving her to the small house next door was the perfect solution. Getting her settled has been a roller coaster of emotions, but slowly we are finding what works and what doesn't. Although it was never our intent to take control of her life, we quickly learned that our fun-loving mother would not be letting go of her independence without a fight!

She is comforted by and grateful for the security of having us next door, but she usually resists our offers to take her on errands, et cetera. When she relies on family for help, she feels less in control of her life. We offered, through our business, to provide in-home care and companionship services, but Mom hired and paid for them on her own. That way she doesn't feel beholden, as she might if it were family.

We asked my brother, who lives outside Australia, to start scheduling his trips home in advance so that Mom always had them to look forward to. Taking into consideration who she had been before physical illness disrupted her active social life, we knew that keeping Mom active and connected would be crucial. So we taught her to use the Internet. She connects with friends now via e-mail and instant messaging. She loves Google and even has a Skype account so that she and my brother can talk face-to-face when he's not here. I'm expecting any day for her to start texting, and when she sends me a friend request on Facebook, I'll know the party animal is back.

But Mom still does get lonely and will allow us to visit her. As long as we are not trying to help or infringing on her high-spirited freedom, she is happy to see us. I joke about it, but I really admire her. She was so angry and depressed after Dad died that I worried we would lose her too. Instead, she fought back and regained a sense of independence through in-home caregiving and adapting to a new lifestyle. This is the upbeat woman I remember, and she is still the heart and soul of any party.

Martin Warner

"Although it was never our intent to take control of her life, we quickly learned that our fun-loving mother would not be letting go of her independence without a fight!"

CAREGIVER'S PRAYER

God of Light and Wisdom,

You have blessed me with a brilliant family. Help me to keep my loved one independent for as long as possible. Please give me the discernment I need to make changes in living situations or daily activities that will help me accomplish this goal. I praise you for the good friend I have in you, Jesus!

"FORE!"

INTRODUCTION

Playing golf requires a lot of time and patience. I tend to get frustrated when I hit a bad shot, or I don't get enough loft and distance on the ball, or miss the ball altogether. I've been known to throw a club or two in a childish fit.

Golf teaches us many life lessons. Unpredictable bounces in our day cause frustration. We take our eyes off the ball and our lives roll into areas we did not intend for them to go. We get off the fairway and get stuck in the rough or a sand trap. It is our responsibility to play the ball where it lands and advance it forward. Who is driving your shots, you or the Lord?

Sarah has learned to overcome her feelings of guilt toward her father and tallies the blessings that come from her love and devotion.

··

INSPIRATIONAL VERSE
Cast all your anxiety on him because he cares
for you.

I PETER 5:7

··

MESSAGE

It has been said that all people will leave a legacy. Something one hands down to those he leaves behind. My father's legacy to my sister and his grandchildren is the game of golf.

Dad was a high school math teacher and coached boys' basketball and golf. He has always been a "man's man," and for some reason God blessed him with three daughters. I often wondered if Dad ever wished for a boy, so I did the best I could by becoming quite the tomboy. I loved hanging out at the gym while he coached, or serving as water girl at football practice.

The first gift I can remember being given to me solely by my father was a sawed-off driver. It was covered with athletic tape (my dad's version of superglue!). In addition to teaching and coaching, Dad held summer jobs, so one-on-one time with him was a precious commodity. I cherished any time with him. His gift of that old driver allowed me to share something with him in a way I never had before. If quality time with Dad meant golf, then I was going to become a golfer!

After reminding my sister and me to keep our eyes on the ball, he'd step back and say, "Let it rip!" Usually we would take a huge divot of grass out of the tee box or miss the ball entirely. But good old Dad never gave up on us. Just being the center of his attention meant the world to both of us.

Time flies, children grow up, move out, get married, and start their own lives. Some forty years later, however, the legacy of golf continues. Only now, our roles have been reversed. My dad, who could once drive a ball three hundred yards, was known as a master chipper and deadeye putter, now has macular degeneration. Instead of me being frustrated because I didn't hit the ball as far as I desired, my father is the frustrated one.

This once proud "man's man" has to rely on his "little girl" to help him on the course. This role reversal is actually bittersweet for me. I love the game; I enjoy spending time with my father; however, it breaks my heart as I watch Dad grow frustrated and angry.

Now I am expected to be his eyes and watch his ball as it sails down the fairway. He can still see well enough to hit the ball, but the disease won't allow him to watch how far or where it goes once he does. He constantly calls out, "You are going to watch this, right?" which makes it hard for me to concentrate on my own game. It's at these moments that I can become very frustrated and want to scream!

But then, like a gentle breeze, the Holy Spirit knocks quietly on my heart to remind me of the patience and love my dad needs. My score then becomes secondary. I shoot up an arrow prayer asking for patience and joy, then I lean over and give my dad a pat on the leg or a slug on the arm to tell him it's okay. We smile and keep on playing. It might be simpler in some ways to let him put the clubs away for good; however, a good caddie never gives up on his player, and I won't give up on Dad!

Wanting to help off the course is a desire as well, but living three hundred miles away from my parents makes that a challenge. Many days I can get sucked under by the guilt avalanche of I-can'ts.

> I can't drive Dad to his doctors appointments.
> I can't be there to give my mom a break.
> I can't make Dad see better.

If I focus on any of these thoughts, they weigh me down like a suit made of lead, heavy, dark, and incapacitating. It does absolutely no good even to go there in my mind. It just produces guilt and condemnation. So instead, I focus on what I *can* do.

> I *can* pick up the phone and speak a word of encouragement, say "I love you," and give the gift of affirmation.
> I *can* pray (for my dad's healing, my mom's patience, and wisdom for his doctors).
> I *can* be forthright in making time to honor my parents with periodic visits.

I have found the greatest way to show Dad my love. It's spelled T-I-M-E. I can't always be there physically, but I'm grateful God is omnipresent. That He beckons me to "cast my care upon Him and to pray." To lighten my burdens upon Him and allow Jehovah Rapha, the healer, to be in charge of my dad.

This makes me feel peace rather than pain, and I gain freedom and joy in realizing I can't and don't have to do it all by myself. In fact, neither God nor my dad expects me to do it all! God is more than able, and I can be free from the guilt.

Macular degeneration may be slowly taking Dad's vision, but his love of the game of golf is something that will be passed down from generation to generation. As my children give their children that first club (athletic tape optional), Dad's legacy will continue. The greatest lesson I learned from my dad is this: It's not how well you score at the game but enjoying the game with the people you love. Now that's a hole in one!

Sarah Nordlund

"But then, like a gentle breeze, the Holy Spirit knocks quietly on my heart to remind me of the patience and love my dad needs."

CAREGIVER'S PRAYER
Lord and Master,

You give us great lessons to learn from games such as golf. Thank you for freeing me from guilt over what I can't do and giving me joy in doing what I can.

RAYS OF LIGHT

INTRODUCTION

It was 1982. I was nineteen years old, and I had two
dreams: to be a professional model and to become
Miss Nebraska USA. I was intrigued by the sequined
gowns, glamour, runway, lights, and the mystique that
surrounded the crown and title. They say beauty is only
skin deep, which I knew and believed, but at nineteen I
didn't care about that. My goal was to be Miss Nebraska
USA! And I achieved it!

It was easy to get caught up in that mind-set and go
after earthly pleasures, but fortunately God revealed to
me true beauty as I encountered godly women who ex-
uded beauty from within. These women truly had an
earnest heart for the Lord; I learned from them that the
runway was God's path, and the lights and glamour,
His glory.

God packages people in different ways. This story
teaches us to take the time to look into people's hearts
to find God's most valuable and precious gifts.

INSPIRATIONAL VERSE

"The Lord does not look at the things man looks at. Man looks at the outward appearance, but the Lord looks at the heart."

1 SAMUEL 16:7

MESSAGE

Kathryn and Estelle were both in their late seventies when I met them. They were widowed sisters, each in need of more care than the other could provide. A friend of my mother's knew them through church and suggested I talk to them about coming in to help them when needed. Little did I know how that opportunity would shape the path my life would follow.

Like most nineteen-year-olds, I had completed one year of college but still didn't have any idea what I wanted to be when I "grew up." I had never really helped care for anyone before but remembered thinking, How tough could two old ladies be? If someone had told my nineteen-year-old self this would be the first step to a lifelong career, I would never have believed them. Not at first anyway.

The lessons I learned during that time with Kathryn and Estelle have served me well throughout my life. First of all, I learned that helping to care for two little old ladies is not as easy as it sounds. Estelle was crippled with arthritis and lived with so much pain that it was sometimes difficult to get along with her. Kathryn was in better physical condition but still very frail. While the sisters had lost many of their physical abilities, they had not lost the ability to speak their minds!

At first everything could only be done *their* way, and they were often critical of my efforts. Despite their objections and opinions, I could see that I was helping to improve the quality of their lives. Those early days with the sisters taught me how to care for people who aren't always the most likable. Eventually, we made it past their initial barriers and natural defenses, and they realized that the way I did some things worked "just as well."

Because of her arthritis, Estelle had become confined to the home she and Kathryn shared. I wanted to do something special for her and decided to take her shopping, which she hadn't been able to do in a long time. In spite of the pain and difficulty getting around, she seemed genuinely happy. However, it wasn't her happiness that I remember from that day. It was the looks on the faces of the people around us and how uncomfortable they seemed. I saw how easily they dismissed Estelle as a person and saw only her disabilities.

Seeing her through the eyes of others and seeing the world through Estelle's eyes that day was my awakening. I felt a deep sense of compassion for Estelle on that outing, and it changed the way I looked at elderly, sick, and disabled people. I had heard my calling and thanked

God for the gift of compassion at such an early stage in my life.

It was that experience, and many others like it, that made me realize that not only did I help care *for* these sisters but also I really cared *about* them. I identified with them as a woman and wanted to give them the care they deserved. Estelle was so much more than the crippling arthritis that others saw. And Kathryn was so much more than a frail old lady.

Caring for these sisters and seeing the dynamic between them gave me a glimpse of their entire lives. They were amazing women, loving sisters and adoring wives, who had both lived rich, full lives. They deeply loved each other and wanted the best care for each other no matter how weak they became.

They taught me that to care for someone you must care for the soul, the person who is still on the inside, regardless of how well or poorly the body has aged. I called Estelle and Kathryn the Ray Girls because their maiden name was Ray. I wrote them from college and stayed in touch with them until their deaths.

I became an RN and worked in many areas of health care during my career, but it has always been caring for the elderly that has tugged at my heart the most. That early experience put me on the path to a fulfilling caregiving career and enriched my life. Estelle and Kathryn opened my heart to the compassion within, and I will never forget the Ray Girls for that.

Geneva Labate

"Those early days with the sisters taught me how to care for people who aren't always the most likable."

CAREGIVER'S PRAYER

God of Beauty and Compassion,

Thank you for revealing my life's purpose. Your ways are always filled with wisdom. Help me see the beauty in all people and not just their outside packaging. Let me see through your eyes, Lord, their true hearts so I may love others as you have loved me.

A LOVER OF LOVE . . .
AND OF JELL-O

INTRODUCTION

Some of my most fond memories of our early years of marriage were sitting around Paul's mother's dining room table with his entire family, enjoying our after-dinner coffee. We would sit for hours laughing and reminiscing about the trouble the boys would get into, the crushes the girls had on certain schoolboys, and what life was like during the Depression as seen through the eyes of Grandma Manhart.

It's a shame we don't take the time to sit and visit the way we used to; our lives have become so fast-paced. We have much to learn from our conversations with our families, especially our elder generation: history, genealogy, wisdom, values, relationships, honesty, integrity, spirituality . . . The list goes on.

Listen to Joe as he tells his story of an Italian family, food, and life lessons.

INSPIRATIONAL VERSE

Since my youth, O God, you have taught me,
and to this day I declare your marvelous
deeds.
Even when I am old and gray,
do not forsake me, O God,
till I declare your power to the next generation,
your might to all who are to come.

PSALM 71:17–18

MESSAGE

My mother was doing exactly what she always did, in good times and in bad. She was standing in the doorway between the kitchen and the dining room, one foot in each room, watching her grandchildren with her right eye and, with her left, watching something that was just about to boil over on the stove. In this case, her left eye was on the after-dinner coffee brewing in the kitchen.

In truth, her grandchildren were now old enough to watch over themselves—especially my daughter, an intensive care nurse who could have had us all feeling like a million bucks if we'd only followed her orders. But our children are our children, and our grandchildren are our grandchildren. And we keep our own counsel when we face decisions of ultimate importance.

At least that's what I was thinking as we were sitting with my father, talking about his illness. He wasn't following anyone's orders anymore.

A series of small strokes had left him thin and unsteady but didn't entirely explain his rapid decline. None of us ever received a satisfactory explanation. I'm certain he didn't really know what was wrong with him either, beyond his advanced years. But he didn't seem to care about a definitive diagnosis. He seemed quite content—disappointingly, maddeningly content—to coast into the hereafter.

For the first time in over a half century of marriage, he wasn't interested in my mother's cooking. All he craved that evening, and for weeks before and after that evening, were sugar wafer cookies and Jell-O.

In a matter of months, my sons-in-law and I would clear my parents' bedroom and carry in a hospital bed, complete with bed rails and hydraulics. The entire apartment would become my father's hospice. But at that moment, the apartment—and particularly the dining room—was still the center of an extended family that had migrated out of Brooklyn and now sprawled across several states. Food and drink were still important to us, especially wine and anything parmigiana. And Jell-O seemed like surrender.

My father was not a quitter, and he was never morbid. He'd survived his parents, several brothers and sisters, and one of his two sons, yet he'd retained a remarkable youthful exuberance into his eighth decade. Perhaps every son reveres his father, but I can say honestly that my father warmed every room he entered. I can say that honestly because that's what everyone always told me, and what I always felt. Constitutionally, philosophically, my father was joyful, sometimes to idiosyncratic extremes.

He was the kind of guy who would continue to wear a WORLD'S GREATEST GRANDFATHER T-shirt long after the clothes dryer had shrunk it to a youth size. "My babies gave it to me" was all he'd say when I averted my eyes from the faded decal stretched across his otherwise elderly torso.

He was the kind of guy who would pinch his wife whenever she walked by, then blow her a kiss and wink at her until she smiled. And then wink at anyone else who'd witnessed his flirtation, until they smiled too.

"I love love!" he'd shout on a Sunday morning. And everyone always knew that he meant it.

He was not the kind of guy who turned his back on life. That was what was so surprising about the Jell-O. It was uncharacteristic of him, just as everything bland was uncharacteristic of him.

So there we were, all of us—except my mother, who was standing in the doorway—sitting at the dining room table, all of us marveling at the change that had come over my father when I asked him the question that had always been foremost in my mind and was, in fact, the entirety of my understanding of life and death: "Dad, aren't you afraid?"

He frowned and actually looked incredulous. "Why should I be?" he asked. "Better people than me have died."

I remember gasping. My wife and kids have told me

that they got goose bumps. Only my mother took it in stride; she nodded at the good sense of my father's outlook, and then went to get the coffee.

My father wasn't much of a churchgoer in his later years, but privately he remained a religious man. And I realize now that this is what religion, and a religious understanding of his own life, had taught him: Death is something we all share. Along with birth, it is the only truly normal and entirely predictable feature of life. And a man who knows who he is, neither the best nor the worst but simply one man among many, has nothing to fear.

I don't think this was a late-in-life revelation for my father. In hindsight, it seems pretty clear that he had come to this conclusion long before he expressed it. He had no illusions about his place in the cosmos. If he'd ever believed himself immortal, he'd stopped believing that long ago. He was a hardworking husband and father, a grandfather in a skintight T-shirt, a lover of love, and he expected no special treatment. And so, he was not afraid.

He was just a guy whose old body was failing him, and he'd developed a taste for Jell-O. And so my mother returned from the kitchen with a bowl of jiggly orange cubes for him, and a cup of coffee for me.

Joe Tessitore

"Death is something we all share. Along with birth, it is the only truly normal and entirely predictable feature of life."

CAREGIVER'S PRAYER

Lord God,

You are the ultimate lover of love. Thank you for the precious gift of family. Help me to pass along the important lessons and promises of your never-ending love, power, and might to our younger generation. Help my family enjoy life to its fullest, if not with great parmigiana, then with soothing Jell-O.

THE HAND WE'RE DEALT

INTRODUCTION

Some years have more than their fair share of natural disasters. Earthquakes, tsunamis, floods, fires, hurricanes, and tornadoes. Natural disasters can leave devastation, despair, and death in their paths and cause many people to worry about and fear for their future. What does God have in store for us next? Why is it that some people are dealt a difficult hand full of trial after trial while others are dealt an easier hand? It seems unfair at times. But fixing our eyes on the Lord, who strengthens our faith and gives us peace, will help us to live one day at a time and not become consumed with worry and fear.

This is a lesson Jean clearly learned from God and shares with others today.

INSPIRATIONAL VERSE

"Therefore do not worry about tomorrow, for tomorrow will worry about itself. Each day has enough trouble of its own."

MATTHEW 6:34

MESSAGE

Caregiving has taught me what it means to give and receive unconditional love. It has also taught me that the only thing any of us can do is play the cards we're dealt, knowing that they've come from the hand of God. He doesn't want us to worry about what might happen tomorrow or wait until we hit the jackpot to rejoice. He wants us to go all in, to live for today and celebrate life in small increments.

I have been the caregiver to a father with Alzheimer's, an aging mother, and a sister with a malignant, inoperable brain tumor. Each experience has been life-changing, but all of them taught me not to live too far out or to get too ahead of myself. It is tempting to wish that time would pass more quickly, but that is a mistake. Living in the here and now and being present for our loved ones, sick or healthy, young or old, is the greatest gift we can give to others and to ourselves.

Sometimes, I wonder what God's plan is that He would allow such illness in our family. But it takes just a quick look around to see that there are people far worse off to put things into perspective. I am fortunate to be in the position to care for my family as they have needed me.

My father, Bob, was an obstetrician, and my mother, JoAnn, was a nurse who helped care for the babies he delivered. They both dedicated their careers to caring for the lives newly brought into the world. I always respected the level of care they provided to their patients, so it was my wish to return to them that level of love and care as they began to age.

Once Dad started suffering from the advanced stages of Alzheimer's, we had to move him to a nursing home because his care began to affect my mom's health. She felt it was her duty to care for him, not only as his wife but because of her career as a nurse; neither oath weakens with age. At the time, my husband and I lived in Connecticut and my parents in Nebraska, so making the decision as a long-distance caregiver to put him in a nursing home was difficult but necessary. Dad would have expected us to make that decision on his behalf.

My father, very gentle by nature, turned combative in the last months of his life. He hadn't been eating like he should, so before I left, I took him a special surprise. It was July 4, and I served him a picnic dinner with the requirement that he clean his plate before he could receive homemade ice cream, his all-time favorite dessert. We had a great time together. Dad may not have been able to remember what was happening day to day, but he could recall events at church fifty years before. I knew as he talked about his childhood church that his heart had always been with God. He and God filled my heart with unconditional love that day. I was at peace as I kissed him good-bye.

Mom now lives in a nursing home because of her declining health. She misses Dad terribly and tells us frequently that she "wants to go be with him in heaven." It is heartwarming to know that love transcends death and that Dad will be there with open arms when it is her time.

In 2010, my sister Linda was diagnosed with an inoperable brain tumor. It was an unbelievable shock. She lived with us during her chemotherapy and radiation, and we witnessed firsthand how cancer affects the people it touches. Having a daughter with a brain tumor has made my mom feel like she "should be the one to go," but Linda has no intentions of going anywhere quite yet. She has beaten the odds and is back home with her family, where she continues to get stronger one day at a time.

None of us knows what cards we will be dealt next. The lesson that I've learned through my caregiving experiences is to have a strong faith in the Lord. It is essential. There is no need to up the ante once you turn yourself over to the unconditional love of God.

Jean Lynn

"Living in the here and now and being present for our loved ones, sick or healthy, young or old, is the greatest gift we can give to others and to ourselves."

CAREGIVER'S PRAYER

Sovereign Watchman,

We know that we are dealt many hands in life that are not pleasant, but we need to play them to the best of our ability. Watch over me and go before me, Lord, to prepare and strengthen me for whatever lies ahead. Remind me to give you all my worries, fears, and doubts because I know you love me unconditionally and you do not want my heart to be troubled. When you are near, Lord, there is nothing to fear.

APRIL FOOLS' DAY

INTRODUCTION

My children successfully played an April Fools' joke on me that worked not only once but twice. They wrapped black electrical tape around the kitchen sink sprayer so that the lever was held down in the ready-to-spray position. Unknowingly, I turned on the water to get a drink and got doused in the face with water. Like a dummy, I did it again, thinking the pressure would somehow unstick the lever. I thought wrong and got doused a second time. The kids were hiding around the corner and blurted out in great delight, *"April Fool."*

Not all April Fools are fun and games. April 1, 2009, is a date I will never forget. On that day my parents frantically called me with the news that my sister's husband, Jim, was in the emergency room at Creighton Hospital because he was having a massive stroke. I thought this couldn't be . . . what a terrible April Fools' joke my brother-in-law was playing on all of us. No joke—this was for real!

Listen to my sister Wendy's story and hear the

desperation in her heart as she suddenly becomes her husband's caregiver.

- -

INSPIRATIONAL VERSE

The Lord is my shepherd, I shall lack
　　nothing.
He makes me lie down in green pastures,
he leads me beside quiet waters,
he restores my soul.
He guides me in paths of righteousness
for his name's sake.
Even though I walk
through the valley of the shadow of death,
I will fear no evil,
for you are with me;
your rod and your staff,
they comfort me.

PSALM 23:1–4

- -

MESSAGE

"Please, God, wrap your healing arms around Jim and make him better. He is so young. I need him! The boys need him!" I frantically prayed while following the ambulance in which my husband lay unconscious.

The wait for the doctors to relay some news seemed like an eternity. Questions raced through my mind. Will he make it? Will he be the same after this? Finally, the first doctor came out and said they had found something. I started to panic inside. That "something" was a massive cerebral stroke. One of the largest they had seen. The doctors had to act quickly. The pressure in Jim's brain was high, and they needed to drill holes in the skull to relieve it.

Days passed, but his brain swelling didn't improve. The neurosurgeon sat my mother, sister-in-law, and me down in a conference room. He explained that my husband of twenty years might not live through this stroke, and if he did, he would never be the same. Chances were he wouldn't walk or talk again.

Scared and nervous, I had to tell our fourteen- and fifteen-year-old sons. The news was heart-wrenching, to say the least. We held one another awhile, cried, and prayed.

On the thirteenth day, when I went to visit Jim after work, I was shocked to see that his eyes were open. He had been in a medically induced coma since the first day. The doctors had slowly woken him up so he could hear me now. My pastor had stopped by, so we held hands and prayed the Lord's Prayer. As we said "Amen," Jim mouthed the word also, a true miracle. I somehow knew things would be okay.

He spent another week in the hospital before moving to rehabilitation for two weeks. This was going to be the real test. Suddenly, I became a caregiver to my husband, doing for him the things I expected to do at age eighty, not at forty-five. I did so many things for Jim; I drove everywhere for four months, walked next to him so he would not fall, waited for him at rehab, assisted with personal care and as he endured bouts of nausea.

Coming home exhausted after a day's work and

then going to the hospital each night made me wonder if I could handle this for the rest of my life if needed. Praying for strength and patience, I often relied on Philippians 4:13: "I can do all things through him who strengthens me." I also knew that God would never give me more than I could handle, so it was time to persevere and move forward.

Jim came home exactly one month after his stroke. He had recovered about ninety percent and only needed a cane to get around. The doctors and therapists called him a walking miracle, and everyone who saw Jim believed them. I was physically, mentally, and emotionally drained but never happier to have him back at home, where he was loved and needed.

Realizing I couldn't take care of Jim and work at the same time, my sister, Lori, cofounder of Home Instead Senior Care, offered a caregiver to help us out for a few weeks. God answers so many prayers, I thought. This was such a blessing and lifted many burdens off my shoulders. Jim had worked two full-time jobs to make ends meet. It was a financial strain to have him out of work for three and a half months. The help of professional caregivers allowed me to work without worries. Jim loved having them around too. He especially enjoyed beating them at cribbage.

What we learned most through this life-changing experience is that you can never underestimate the power of prayer, faith, and the support of family and friends. Without any one of these components, we could not have made a full recovery.

Wendy Kuhn

"Suddenly, I became a caregiver to my husband, doing for him the things I expected to do at age eighty, not at forty-five."

CAREGIVER'S PRAYER

God of Miracles,

All of a sudden, I'm a caregiver because of an unexpected illness. I'm afraid of what lies ahead, but you tell me not to fear, for you are with me. I know that you will give me strength to make it through the vast unknown. Thank you for being with me every step of the way to guide me and to reassure me of your love and faithfulness. I'm thankful that you are in the business of making miracles happen every day.

HE WILL NOT FAIL ME

INTRODUCTION

Paul's mother, Catherine, raised three boys and three girls all by herself. Paul was the third child. Catherine was a great seamstress and had several paying jobs to make ends meet; she made draperies for interior designers, sewed school uniforms, and did small tailoring jobs for families in the neighborhood. Catherine eventually owned her own maid service, which put the last child through college. I greatly admired Catherine for the work ethic she instilled in her children and the closeness they shared as a family.

When we started Home Instead, in 1994, Catherine was quick to offer us her living room to convert into our first office. The arrangement worked out well because it enabled Paul to keep a close eye on Grandma Manhart during the day, while Catherine worked. Catherine had invited Grandma to live with her for what she thought would be the last year of Grandma's life.

Now I'll let Catherine tell her story of how she helped Grandma Manhart regain the will to live.

INSPIRATIONAL VERSE

But the fruit of the Spirit is love, joy, peace, patience, kindness, goodness, faithfulness, gentleness and self-control.

GALATIANS 5:22

MESSAGE

Mother came to live with me when she was ninety years old. She had twelve children, fifty grandchildren, and fifty-one great-grandchildren, so although she lived in my home, there was never a lack of support or care from her family. As the matriarch of our big family, Eleanor was surrounded with love and deep respect as she lived to be just shy of 101 years old.

At that time, it was expected that children take care of their parents. My brothers, sister, and I never felt like we were doing anything extraordinary. It was our job to take care of Mother, and that's what we did. She didn't require much care prior to her nineties, but we all did whatever we could to keep her comfortable and safe in her home. Well before we moved her to my house, we had established a culture of caregiving within our family, which made decisions easier. Caring for Mother was a collaborative effort. She made it a joyful and pleasurable experience, even when we were faced with tougher decisions.

My sister and I found out that Mother had not been eating, and the lack of nourishment was beginning to take its toll on her health. She originally resisted the idea of moving in with any of us, but once she was here, she liked it. I still worked full-time, so she continued to be alone during the day until she was ninety-eight years old. My home was the most logical choice because I was single but also because I lived in her neighborhood. This allowed Mother to stay within a familiar environment and remain at the parish she loved. She flourished. Had she been yanked from her neighborhood and lost her sense of community, the outcome may not have been as positive.

Even though she was familiar with the neighborhood, Mother still had to learn to live in a new home. We had to teach her when not to answer the door. We brought in a stair lift to help her get to her bedroom. She took all the changes in stride. My sisters and brothers created a calendar of chores and split the duties. It wasn't easy, but it wasn't hard either; it just took organization.

Shortly after the move, Mother fell while bending over to get the newspaper. We had no idea how long she had been lying there, bleeding and in need of stitches. When her grandson later saw her black eyes and asked what happened, she just winked and said, "You should see the other guy." That easygoing nature and sense of humor were intact until the day she died.

Caring for Mother during the last decade of her life taught me many lessons, not the least of which is that aging is a positive thing. Because of her example, none of her children are afraid to age or to die. She attended church every day, and we said the Rosary daily as a family. She instilled in us such a deep faith in God that I knew He would never fail us as we were called upon to care for her.

Although she was soft-spoken, Eleanor Manhart was highly social and loved people. Another lesson she taught by her example was to live to the very end. Don't let "being too old" limit you. When Mother was eighty-six years old, she went to Europe with my sister, who is a nun and a nurse, and my brother who is a priest. She saw everything she had ever read about or wanted to see. My sister and brother would try to get her to rest in the hotel, but she wouldn't hear of it—wherever they went, she went too. She came home glowing and spoke about that trip for the rest of her life.

The last image I have of Mother is her in her chair in the sitting room, where she loved to knit, read, and tell stories to her grandchildren. It was her favorite place. Passing away during an after-dinner nap in that chair was a beautiful way for her to go.

Mother lived and loved fully and continues to have a positive influence on the lives of her children and grandchildren. Although I had a strong sense of responsibility to care for her, she truly made doing the job one of the great joys of my life.

Catherine Hogan

> *"Another lesson she taught by her example was to live to the very end. Don't let 'being too old' limit you."*

CAREGIVER'S PRAYER

Divine Lord,

Your goodness and blessings are abundant. Thank you for allowing our family to care for Mother at home, where she wants to live out her years. Keep me strong and faithful in my promise to love and serve her each day. I know you will not fail me. Thank you for the privilege of making a difference in her life and helping her regain the will to live. My joy is in you, O Lord; you have made my joy complete.

GOD IS GOOD
AND DOES RIGHT

INTRODUCTION

Twenty-five years ago I said "I do" to my wonderful husband, Paul, and vowed to be his faithful wife to have and to hold, for better, for worse, for richer, for poorer, in sickness and in health, to love and to cherish till death do us part. Those vows resonated in my head as I read Jim's touching story of his beautiful bride of thirty-two years.

INSPIRATIONAL VERSE

Love is patient, love is kind. It does not envy, it does not boast, it is not proud. It is not rude, it is not self-seeking, it is not easily angered, it keeps no record of wrongs. Love does not delight in evil but rejoices with the

> truth. It always protects, always trusts, al-
> ways hopes, always perseveres.
>
> I CORINTHIANS 13:4–7

MESSAGE

*How do I tell the woman who has been my best friend,
constant companion, lover, greatest supporter, and deepest confidante that it's time to give up a fight that she
cannot win? How do I deal with the loss as I see the hope
for life drain out of her eyes? I can't ever remember speaking more difficult or damaging words to anyone than I
did last night to the one person who has been a part of
my life for thirty-two years. In taking away her hope for
life I felt more evil than the cancer that's inside of her.*

*In a few hours the hospice people will be here. And I
suppose that we will formally begin the process of dying,
which in truth has probably been all but inevitable from
the first moment we learned there was cancer in her body.*

From an e-mail dated February 8 to family and friends
just eight days before my beautiful Diana stepped into
eternity.

I will never, ever forget that dreadful moment when I
told my wife there was no hope of a cure for the cancer
that had been attacking her body. She had been sleeping

that evening just as she did most of the time toward the end. When Diana woke up, our family—our two daughters, our son, and I—gathered around her, and her death sentence came out of my mouth: "Honey, the doctors want to stop the chemotherapy. There is no hope." As I watched the hope drain from her eyes, she sagged in the recliner and said, "So, they're giving up on me." That was it. Nothing more. But over the eight days that remained of her life, I witnessed her wage a heroic—albeit hopeless—effort to overcome the devil cancer that had invaded her body.

It seemed that our fight had begun only moments earlier. But in fact it had been six weeks since the totally unexpected diagnosis had thrust our family and my life into an unanticipated, unfamiliar, and frightening new world. One moment we were a happy family, optimistic about the future. The next all those hopes had vanished. Our dreams were shattered. Our lives were turned upside down. What had once seemed important suddenly became trivial. We had become caregivers, thrust into an unwanted world of unfamiliar medical terms and new responsibilities. We learned quickly to become caregivers. After all, we had to help manage Diana's care.

She would live for only six weeks after diagnosis, but at that time we had no way of knowing the brevity and intensity of our caregiving responsibilities. Looking back I see that, of all we dealt with, the most difficult thing was the helplessness, hopelessness, and desperation of our situation. From the moment of diagnosis, it was clear that there was no hope for a cure.

And many times I found myself prostrate on the floor, crying out to God to heal my beloved wife, but deep inside knowing that would never happen.

Yet in spite of that, I clung to a promise: "The Lord is good and does what is right." These few words from Psalm 25:8 (NLT) gave me the hope that somehow God was going to bring good out of what I could see only as a desperately bad situation. I clung to those words. They were my lifeline. Deep inside I knew that God by His very nature is good and that, being good, He could only do good. So I knew that, somehow, God was going to bring good out of this terrible circumstance.

This hope sustained me through six weeks of caregiving. Through emotional ups and downs. Through brief improvements in Diana's condition and heartwrenching relapses. Through the seemingly endless caregiving and the hours at her side in the hospital. Through feelings of the deepest guilt that this devil cancer could have advanced so far without our knowing about it when there still may have been time for a cure. Through the darkest times when I pondered making just one more effort to find a cure, no matter how desperate it might be—a trip to Mexico, a holistic diet, anything. And through the shame that I didn't make that one last effort that may have saved her life.

Through all of this and more, I kept clinging to that one promise—that God is good and does right. It was what sustained me and gave me hope.

When the end came, it came quickly. I had tucked Diana into "her" bed, a hospital bed positioned at the foot of our bed. I read her the get-well cards she had received that day. And I told her that I loved her. "I love you too," she responded. Those were the last words she ever spoke. I woke up at 3:00 A.M. Her breathing was irregular. She was unresponsive. And a few hours later she slipped into eternity with her family gathered around her.

My life, my plans, my hopes and dreams died with my wife. But while I could not imagine what good could come from this circumstance, I continued to cling to that promise: God is good and does right. It sustained me in the hard months that followed.

Dear Friends,

Diana's struggle is over. While some may say she died, she has never been more alive.

For all your prayers and your support and your encouragement, we extend our most heartfelt appreciation.

From a final e-mail to friends dated February 16.
Jim Beck

"Through all of this and more, I kept clinging to that one promise—that God is good and does right. It was what sustained me and gave me hope."

CAREGIVER'S PRAYER

Blessed Redeemer,

Life gets so hard at times and it's difficult to press on, especially when we must go on alone. Help me to turn my feelings of helplessness, hopelessness, and desperation over to your hands because I cannot deal with it all right now. It comforts me to know that you are with me every step of the way, assuring me of your love and embracing me when my circumstances get unbearable. You know my future, and I can safely place my trust and hope in you. You are good, God, and you do right.

BUTTERFINGERS

INTRODUCTION

Have you ever gotten the giggles during church? My grandpa Novicki got my sister Wendy (whom he jokingly called Gabby because she rarely said a word) and me in trouble with our mother at a great-aunt's funeral because we burst out laughing. Gramps was sitting directly in front of us. Our mother didn't know it, but Gramps was folding his huge left ear, which was obviously quite spongy, into his inner ear, where it disappeared for a few seconds. He then wiggled his forehead. And *boing!* His ear popped out again. It was the funniest thing we had ever seen Gramps do! How does one discover that he has this kind of talent in the first place? Gramps had always been a gruff Polish man, and we were quite frankly afraid of him . . . until that moment. Then we discovered he was nothing but an old teddy bear with very flexible ears. I got to appreciate a side of Gramps that I had never before seen. A side that was ornery and unpredictable.

Alzheimer's revealed a different side of Dan's father.

Instead of trying to find the man they once knew, Dan's family embraced the man that he had become.

··

INSPIRATIONAL VERSE
Teach the older men to be temperate, worthy of respect, self-controlled, and sound in faith, in love and in endurance.

TITUS 2:2

··

MESSAGE

Caregiving is a little like walking into the shallow end of a pool; before you realize how far you've gone, you find yourself in the deep end, only you don't know how deep it really is. The commitment of caregiving increases over time. Helping with one thing leads to helping with another. Before you know it, a caregiver is born. The flip side is that caregiving often ends more abruptly than it begins. You adjust to losing your personal time, but it is also an adjustment when you suddenly get your life back.

It's the stuff that happens between getting in over your head and returning to your "normal" life that makes caregiving such a worthwhile endeavor. So, even though I have thus far compared caregiving to being in over your head and having your social life take a significant hit, I don't regret a single moment spent caring for those I love.

My mother, Ann, cared for my father, John, in their home for three years after he was diagnosed with Alzheimer's. Mom would care for Dad during the day, and

I or one of my sisters would go over after work to relieve Mom so she could do her own running around.

I liked taking Dad to run errands as a way to get him out of the house. One day we filled the truck with gas and went inside to pay. I asked Dad if there was anything he wanted, but he said no and stood by me in line. That was when this seemingly mundane errand turned into a priceless memory.

There on the counter was a box of Butterfinger candy bars, his all-time favorite treat. He was eyeing the box but said he didn't want one. I looked away for a moment, only to turn around and catch Dad sliding a Butterfinger into his coat pocket! Shoplifting candy bars from the Kwik Shop was not part of my father's MO, and yet there he was, caught red-handed.

I felt like a parent who could barely contain laughter as his child misbehaves in the most hilarious way. I told Dad if he wanted a Butterfinger, all he had to do was ask, but he could not just put one in his pocket without paying. Dad stood there for a few moments with the orneriest look on his face, as if contemplating whether the fun of misbehaving outweighed the possible punishment. He then picked up three Butterfingers and shoved them into his mouth, wrappers and all. Astonished, embarrassed, and nearly exploding with laughter, I turned to the clerk and told him we'd also be taking three Butterfingers.

One evening when I stopped at my folks' house Mom warned me that it had been "one of those days." Dad would get into silent moods, not looking at or talking to Mom for the entire day. We had not lost him completely. He still had days when he was lucid and responsive; so the silent days caused Mom to worry that he was slipping away entirely. I told her to get out of the house, clear her head, and have some fun. There was a baseball game on, so if Dad wanted to watch the game and not talk, that was fine with me.

An hour or so of complete silence had passed before he turned to me and said, "Where's my Butterfinger?" When Mom came home, I assured her that he was still in there as we laughed about the only three words he spoke all day. On my way home, I was in a drive-thru for a quick sandwich when it occurred to me that if Dad were to die overnight his last spoken word would be "Butterfinger." By the time I reached the window for my food, I was laughing and crying at the same time. Great, yet another clerk who thinks I'm crazy!

I circled back to my parents' house. Dad had gone to bed, but I went upstairs to wake him and tell him that I loved him. I asked him if he loved me too so that those words would be his last, if he were suddenly to die.

Three days after my parents' forty-fifth wedding anniversary, we had to move Dad into a hospice facility. Medicare patients must be transported by ambulance rather than by family, so at the scheduled time, an ambulance arrived. No sirens, no fire truck following behind, just a quiet, routine house call. Although we were all keenly aware that he was leaving home for the last time, Dad thought he was just going for a ride. He was smiling and waving good-bye as they wheeled him into the ambulance.

All five of us children and our mother were able to be with him when he passed two weeks later. There was a sense of relief as we made it back to the shallow end of the pool, but we missed caring for the man we had always known and the ornery and unpredictable man he had become in those last years.

Dan Wieberg

> *"It's the stuff that happens between getting in over your head and returning to your 'normal' life that makes caregiving such a worthwhile endeavor."*

CAREGIVER'S PRAYER

Lord of All,

Help me to be flexible and have the ability to go with the flow as I care for my parent with Alzheimer's. I pray that I will not get angry when things don't go as planned throughout the day. Help me to discover the humor in unusual situations and not take life so seriously. But most of all, Lord, I want my parent to know he is loved. Thank you for your tender, unconditional love.

DEFYING ALL ODDS

INTRODUCTION

My girlfriend, Kim, lives up the street from me and has four children, two of whom are twins with cerebral palsy. To say they have a few challenges is an understatement. Her husband and children are strong Christians and rely on the Lord for His help and provision. Kim's faith has been an inspiration and encouragement to me. She is a beautiful example of how a Godly woman reacts in times of crisis or challenge; she gets down on her knees, prays, and searches the Scriptures for answers.

In the same way, Tracy places herself before the Lord and asks Him to walk her through times of joy and times of adversity.

Speak up and judge fairly;
defend the rights of the poor and needy.
PROVERBS 31:8–9

MESSAGE

After five years of fertility treatments, pregnancy was
only the first of our blessings. Julia was sent directly from
God. He entrusted us to care for this angel, initially disguised as a fussy baby who seemed defensive and combative when touched and held. She was easily bothered
by noises and made random movements that we didn't
know weren't normal.

My daughter Julia was born with multiple disabilities and lissencephaly, an extremely rare brain forma-
tion disorder. Many doctors immediately wrote her off.
Perhaps in an effort to prepare us for her imminent
death, they began sentences with phrasings such as
"When you have another child . . ." One doctor even
went so far as to tell us that "Julia is not compatible for
life." After her diagnosis, we were told she had "possibly two years," but evidently God and Julia had much
different plans. Twenty years later, Julia still doesn't know
that she and life are "incompatible."

The doctors were right when they told us our "other
children" would not suffer from the same disabilities.
My husband, Terry, and I were blessed with two more
beautiful children, Brian and Christy. We've learned that
caring for anyone, disabled or not, brings its own unique
challenges. Julia, Brian, and Christy are all children of

God; Julia's disabilities are God's purposeful design in the exact way that Brian's and Christy's abilities were carefully designed by His hand. Julia's disabilities were not a mistake; she is exactly as Lord Jesus intended her to be.

There have been waves of chronic grief for the child we thought we'd have, for the life we dreamed of, and for having to live with the knowledge that Julia may die at any time. But God didn't promise us it would be easy. He did promise that He'd walk beside us, grieve with us, and celebrate with us. His eternal light overshadows our chronic grief with the chronic joy of living life to its fullest. With His guidance, we live every day as the gift it was intended to be.

Our lives have certainly been affected by the structure and requirements needed to care for Julia. In the early days, doctors left us to learn about her disease on our own. We've lost friends who couldn't handle it, yet our lives continue to be full of wonderful people who can. We wouldn't have chosen this life, but we have chosen to do our best to honor this precious gift from Jesus.

Terry and I praise God for the lessons He teaches through Julia. She inspires us to value people, not for what they do, but simply because they are His wonderfully made creations. Her disabilities give her a purity that keeps her so close to God's image that she remains untainted by outside stresses and burdens. Time with Julia strips away all the material layers of life, exposing God's unconditional love. She teaches us that the only thing that matters is who we love, and who loves us.

After twenty years, Julia continues to defy the odds. Most days all we can do for Julia is keep her comfortable. We are fortunate to have a small team of professional caregivers to assist us when needed. We all truly believe Julia offers more care for our souls than any of us could ever provide for her body.

Julia cannot tell her own story; so Terry and I are not only her parents and caregivers but also her advocates. Brian and Christy are her biggest fans. If we can advance her mission to inspire others to learn that with God anything is possible, then we will be fulfilled. Her messages are simple and pure: Never judge another based on abilities or disabilities, and physical appearance simply never matters. Every life is a worthy endeavor and a wonderful gift.

Tracy Baugh

"She inspires us to value people, not for what they do, but simply because they are His wonderfully made creations."

CAREGIVER'S PRAYER

Lord of Justice and Peace,

Just like in the poem "Footprints in the Sand" by

Mary Stevenson, you are always walking beside me, and you carry me through the rough times in my life. Thank you for your Holy Scriptures that guide and direct my steps. Give me the boldness to speak up for those who cannot speak for themselves, the compassion to judge fairly, and the insight to see the gold gleaming beneath the brass.

THE LAST OF THE
GOLDEN GIRLS

INTRODUCTION

The kids are starting to leave home. Two are in college and the other two are rarely around anymore—off at school, at work, or hanging with friends. They are all self-sufficient; even the youngest is now driving. I feel as though they don't need me as much; it's a sad feeling and a great feeling at the same time. (Excuse me while I have my own little pity party for just a moment.) I guess I didn't realize how much I enjoyed being needed by my family. I'm sure most mothers feel the same way about their children.

I can identify with Rae as her aunt stops needing the assistance she once relied upon.

INSPIRATIONAL VERSE

You turned my wailing into dancing;

you removed my sackcloth and clothed me
    with joy,

that my heart may sing to you and not be
    silent.

O Lord my God, I will give you thanks for-
    ever.

PSALM 30:11–12

MESSAGE

A woman of a certain age, still fashionably dressed, hair coiffed, nails polished, her makeup perfect: Aunt Mary and her younger sister, who lived together in their later years, were dubbed the Golden Girls by the family. One year ago on Palm Sunday, my aunt Mary was getting dressed, carefully selecting the accessories for her going-to-church outfit, when she fell. She was on the floor in her bedroom with a broken hip and, for the first time, in need of help.

It was during those months when she was hospitalized and in rehab that our relationship became clearly defined in a way that surprised me. Doctors, nurses, and staff began to assume that I was her daughter. Aunt Mary is my confirmation godmother, but it became clear that our relationship had evolved to the point where she regarded me as her daughter.

My aunt was an independent business owner and had lived in the same place in Brooklyn for most of her life. She was no longer able to live alone and no longer self-sufficient. She is not able to walk to the stores, church, or beauty shop as she had always done. Her children, Joe and Donna, found a perfect care facility, close enough so that they could get there in minutes in case of an emergency. I would no longer have to brave the freeway, bridges, and tunnels of New York to see her; I could reach her via a pleasant fifty-minute drive on backcountry roads from Connecticut to Northern Westchester. It was a life transition for Aunt Mary. But it is coming up on one year since she relocated, and her story is telling. Like children, the elderly can often be far more resilient than we expect.

I always phoned Aunt Mary the day before I planned to visit to get a list of what she might need me to bring and to remind her that I would pick her up at the usual time for our shopping trip and lunch. I got a call from her that night saying I should postpone my visit to the day after tomorrow. Her residence was having a Mardi Gras party the following evening. Lions Club members were coming, and there would be a live orchestra with dancing. Like any true Golden Girl, she wanted to look her best; she had her hair touched up and her nails done, and she needed time to choose the right outfit.

I visited the day after the soiree and found her in one of the community rooms with the group. She waved me in and said, "There's a seat in the back, just sit and join us. We are watching the pictures from last night's Mardi Gras party." When the slide show was over, Aunt Mary said that she wanted to see it again and that I should wait for her in her room. I was not surprised to see that there were some sweet photos of her dancing with some of the men from the Lions Club. Aunt Mary was never the type to sit on the sidelines and watch, so broken hip or not, her dance card had been full.

As I was walking toward her apartment, I met the director of the facility, and she saw from the look on my face that I was quite perplexed by the fact that my aunt remained in the room with the others. Her normal response whenever I'd visit was to say, "Hurry up, let's get out of here." The director put her hand on my shoulder and with a knowing smile said, "You're dismissed, she's home now."

Rae Fischetti

> "It was during those months when she was hospitalized and in rehab that our relationship became clearly defined in a way that surprised me."

CAREGIVER'S PRAYER

Caring God,

My senior loved one is doing much better, and I am glad for her good health, but help me adjust to my feelings of not being needed right now. Lord, help me not to dread my golden years but to look forward to them with vim and vigor just like my aunt. I ask you to watch over her and keep her safe and independent until she needs me again.

LOVE STORY

INTRODUCTION

I always find it so interesting to learn how couples met. It was a sorority sister of mine dating a high school buddy of Paul's who set us up on a blind date. I knew nothing about Paul Hogan except that our friends told me he was a "nice guy." I did not know what kind of family he came from, what neighborhood he lived in, what make of car he drove, or if he was an athlete or a computer whiz. Actually, it was quite refreshing to get to know someone and formulate my own opinions instead of relying upon other people's preconceived ideas. Now every time I see Paul's buddy, I tell him *thank you* for setting us up on that initial blind date!

Rob describes the courtship between his grandparents and their continued love story.

INSPIRATIONAL VERSE

Husbands, love your wives, just as Christ loved the church and gave himself up for her.

EPHESIANS 5:25

MESSAGE

If you ask my grandfather how long he and Grandma were married, he'll smile and say "sixty-two years, four months, and two days. It was the easiest sixty-two years of my life." Grandpa is now eighty-seven years old and showing signs of dementia. We lost Grandma three years ago, and although she never set foot in the assisted living apartment where he lives, you feel her presence everywhere. After sixty-two years of marriage, wherever he goes, she will be there too.

Their love story is one for the ages. They met in the Navy shipyard where they both worked. A young woman named Teresa had decided, just the day before meeting this young sailor Bob, that she never wanted to get married. Bob was shipping out for two weeks but asked her if she would go out with him the night he returned. They knew on their second date that they wanted to have six children. That same evening they saw hanging in the window of a store on a street in Boston the wedding dress that Teresa would soon wear. After a two-week courtship and a six-month deployment, they got married and never looked back.

She was seven years older than he, and Grandpa says Grandma started telling him what to do the first day they met and never stopped. She insisted he get a college education so that he could take care of her when she got old. He says that she was the key to every aspect of his success and that she was the one who always took care of him.

Grandma had Alzheimer's, and Grandpa was going to take care of her as she had told him he would need to do someday. Grandpa did everything he could for her, even putting her clothes on her in the right order. More than once she would put her brassiere on last, over all her other clothing. Grandpa tried his best to give her instructions, and she tried her best to obey, but he chuckles now as he says: "Following orders was never in her nature. God bless her!"

They had one year at home together before Grandma fell and had to be moved to a care facility. This was during the time that Sandra Day O'Connor's husband was in the advanced stages of Alzheimer's and living in a care facility. Grandpa remembered reading that Justice O'Connor had followed the doctors' advice to give her husband time to settle into his new home. When she went back to visit him, he had fallen in love with someone else. Grandpa said there was no way he was going to let that happen. He spent every day with Grandma so she'd never have the chance to forget him.

Grandpa is starting to lose his short-term memory, but he remembers every detail of their love story. Regardless of where his mind or memory may travel, he speaks of Grandma with complete devotion. When an eighty-seven-year-old man breaks down in tears because he misses his wife so dearly, you know that he couldn't forget her if he tried; she is in his heart, not his head. And at heart Grandpa is still that twenty-year-old sailor who can't wait to get back to shore and take that beautiful girl out on dates for the next sixty-two years, four months, and two days.

Rob Shradar

"Grandpa said there was no way he was going to let that happen. He spent every day with Grandma so she'd never have the chance to forget him."

CAREGIVER'S PRAYER

Dear God,

You are a jealous, loving God. You want to be the focus of all our praise and worship. Thank you for giving me wonderful grandparents who modeled a great marriage full of love and devotion, patience and perseverance. Help me to keep my loved one's memory alive in my heart and in the hearts of our family for generations to come. Let me follow your perfect example of how we are to love one another—as much as Christ loved the church.

THE HANDS OF TIME

INTRODUCTION

It seems like just yesterday that I was strolling down the aisles of the grocery store with my new baby girl, Lakelyn. Several grandmothers stopped to admire her beauty and told me to cherish every moment of my time with her because babies grow up so fast. When we are new parents, we are so eager for our children to advance to the next stage of development, whether that is eating baby food, taking those first steps, or saying "Dada." Now that baby girl has graduated from college and is ready to step out into the real world and start a career, pay rent, and eventually choose a husband. Sometimes I wish I could turn back the hands of time and recapture some of those precious early moments, but I realize there are many more stages to look forward to in my children's lives, and I want to savor each moment.

Les and his wife, Roberta, remind us to slow down and appreciate the time we have with our loved ones today.

INSPIRATIONAL VERSE

This is the day the Lord has made;
let us rejoice and be glad in it.

PSALM 118:24

MESSAGE

Of all the possible afflictions that a ninety-two-year-old may have to contend with, I never imagined that my mother, Eleanor, would suffer from a self-diagnosed case of the I-can'ts. Her list of constant complaints is growing, and it seems that she has tendered her resignation: "I just can't do it anymore." There are minor health issues, but for her, aging is far more mental than it is physical. She believes that she cannot fight back, and that attitude is having the most negative impact on her quality of life.

Eleanor has been many things during her life: an actress, a Vegas showgirl, a wife, a mother, and an amazing daughter and caregiver for her own mother. Through it all, she was never negative or depressed. Her training as a 1940s Las Vegas showgirl taught her always to smile and hold her head high. That's the Mom I remember, the one whose smile illuminated the room and who carried herself with such confidence and grace that you couldn't help but notice.

Mom is still a beautiful woman, but I think she misses the vibrant girl of days past. It's hard to believe that she has changed so much and it's even more difficult for her to reconcile the differences between the exciting life she once had and the limited freedoms of a ninety-two-year-old. She was always active and independent, so it's understandable that she sometimes wishes she could turn the clock back a bit. Don't we all, from time to time, wish for that?

The primary caregiving responsibilities of my grandmother rested on my mom's shoulders until she herself was eighty and my grandmother was one hundred years old. I've always seen my mom as a woman who could handle anything, but vibrant or not, being a full-time caregiver at the age of eighty must have been a big strain on her. If it was, none of us knew it. To her, it was her duty but also her honor to keep Grandma at home until she passed away. I feel just as honored to do the same for my mom now, but it took an intervention for me to see that she too needed care and companionship.

For many years I played the role of long-distance caregiver, with Mom in California and my family and me in North Carolina. We honestly believed that she would be happy to be living on her own after Grandma died. I remember thinking, Finally she doesn't have anyone to take care of—without considering that Mom might herself be in need of some care. Distance makes it easy to see only what you want to see, and denial is a comfortable place to be. I'm not sure if it was so much denial as it was simply avoidance.

It wasn't that I didn't want to care for Mom; I just wasn't ready to face the changes required in my own life to do so. My cousins, who lived near Mom and saw her almost daily, lovingly communicated with us that

Mom needed more help than she was letting us know. Until then it had been easy to believe Mom's statement, "I'm fine," because I really wanted her to be "fine." But quickly after the conversation with my cousins, we reorganized our lives (and a few priorities) and asked Mom to come live with us.

Living together for this first time in over forty years has in many ways turned the clock back for Mom and me. My wife, Roberta, and I love having her here, even though it has been the toughest journey we have ever been on. I am in the caregiving business and witness firsthand the challenges families face, yet I still could not have foreseen how difficult it would be to balance Mom's needs with our own. It takes extraordinarily hard work to be a caregiver, a husband, and a business owner. I learned from the best showgirl that it's important to hold my head high and to keep smiling.

I am sad to see Mom struggle to embrace fully where she is in her life now. In addition to her physical needs, Mom's spirit is in need of some repair; so we are caring for her soul as well as her body. She is amazingly astute and can't understand why she is aging like this. We've turned to her doctor and physical therapist and other outside influences to help instill in her the belief that she can get stronger and keep living a full life. Sometimes motivation from outside sources is far more effective because it is not taken as criticism.

In our professional and personal lives, my wife and I know the importance of keeping seniors mobile and social. Once those two things go, it's hard to stay engaged and find the strength to keep going. It might be a stretch to make Mom's life quite as exciting as it was under the bright Vegas lights, but Roberta and I are committed to making her feel happy and beautiful again. I hope we have as much time together as Mom had with Grandma. Difficult or not, this is time that we will never get back.

Les Farnum

> *"It wasn't that I didn't want to care for Mom; I just wasn't ready to face the changes required in my own life to do so."*

CAREGIVER'S PRAYER

Timeless Lord,

You tell us that we are but a mist that appears for a little while and then vanishes. Let me rejoice in each new day that you have made and make every moment count. Please enrich the time I have left with my loved one and help me create good memories that our family can share.

MY WIFE IS A SAINT

INTRODUCTION

I once asked Paul's grandmother what she thought was the most valuable piece of advice she could give me for my family. She was surprised that I would even ask her opinion. Grandma Manhart was a devout Catholic and had twelve children, fifty grandchildren, and fifty-one great-grandchildren. I figured she had learned a thing or two over the years and could write a book about all her wisdom, perhaps volumes. She finally told me, "Patience." That's all she said. Patience. As I raise my four children and experience times of frustration, I hear her sweet voice in my head say "patience," and that helps me through every situation. God's Word is like that too. God whispers precious verses when we need help the most. He equips us with relevant Scripture—the living, breathing Word of God, to give us hope and peace.

Joe and his wife, Sandy, believe caregiving is a special privilege. They rely on their faith and prayer to help them through some difficult days.

MESSAGE

My wife, Sandy, cared for my mother, who was suffering from cancer and Alzheimer's. She got a call from her friend who was moving to a retirement community and had to downsize. Among the possessions she was giving away were a dozen life-size vintage statues of saints that she and her son had rescued from a church dumpster forty years ago—like St. Thérèse, St. Anthony, St. Anne, and St. Joseph—which had been thrown out because the church was "modernizing."

For years my mother stored the statues in a shed. Their paint was peeling, their plaster was chipped, and fingers were missing, but she was committed to preserving them. She couldn't take these statues with her, so she called her relatives and friends, hoping they might adopt them.

When Sandy arrived, only two were left, and it was obvious she was meant to take them. One was a four-foot-tall statue of St. Jude, and the other was a life-size statue of St. Anne with the Virgin Mary. My wife was born on St. Jude's feast day, and the aunt who raised her and loved her was named Anne.

St. Anne stayed in our garage until I found a Ukrainian man who worked with icons and could restore her. In a couple of weeks she looked as good as new and occupied a place of honor in our living room.

Sandy had cared for many elderly people in her work as a nurse's aide and in her church ministry with the elderly, sick, and dying. Her philosophy was simple: Never consider the care of a loved one or patient a chore, burden, or obligation but rather a God-given privilege.

She considered caring for my mother a very special privilege, which helped her to get through some pretty difficult days. My daughters and I can attest that Sandy isn't the most patient person in the world, and she admitted, "I always prayed for patience and in caring for Mom I realized that God doesn't give you patience—only the opportunities to be patient. When you care for someone who has Alzheimer's, patience is so important."

Sandy took excellent care of my mother physically as well as spiritually. "Praying the Rosary and Chaplet of the Divine Mercy are some of my fondest memories of our time together," she recalled. In spite of her advanced Alzheimer's, my mother never forgot any of her prayers.

Every morning Sandy would pray for my mother. At first, Sandy asked for a miraculous cure, but later she prayed for simpler needs: that my mother would recover from an infection, that she might get a good night's sleep, and most important, that her death would be a peaceful one.

"I always tried to bring Mom laughter, joy, peace, and hope. Since laughter is the best medicine, we watched countless hours of *I Love Lucy* reruns and laughed hysterically," she recalled. "A person can't live without hope—even if it's the hope of seeing just one more sunrise or sunset. Mom was a woman of extraordinary hope and acceptance of God's will for her life. That's why she outlived all her doctors' predictions."

Six years before, they had told us my mother was "terminally ill" and had only a few months to live. But God had plans of His own.

During her years of caring for the elderly, Sandy also learned that dying people can have deep spiritual experiences, and when you're with them, you are often in the presence of heaven as their loved ones and friends come to bring them home. "It's important to remember you may be caring for a saint, and when they get to heaven, they'll surely put in a good word for you."

Because of Alzheimer's, my mother didn't realize where she was, and whenever she said that she wanted to go home, Sandy would respond, "But, Mom, you are in your home. This is your room, your bed, your house."

Before my mother died, Sandy realized that what she meant by "home" was her heavenly home. Toward the end of Mom's life, it became very difficult, and for the last seventy-four days, my mother wouldn't eat, so Sandy had to spoon-feed her Gatorade.

Then, on a beautiful morning in July, knowing that Mom's death was near, we sat by her bed and prayed that she would have a peaceful death. Sandy held my mother's hand and said, "Mom, all of heaven is here to take you home. I love you. You can go home."

A few moments after we finished praying, she died.

It was a peaceful death. We had been given a gift. It was July 26, the feast day of St. Anne.

Joe Pisani

> *"Her philosophy was simple: Never consider the care of a loved one or patient a chore, burden, or obligation but rather a God-given privilege."*

CAREGIVER'S PRAYER

Father in Heaven,

You tell us to ask and we shall receive. I am asking for patience in dealing with my parent with Alzheimer's. I know you will give me plenty of opportunities to practice my patience, but please give my heart joy and compassion as I minister to her daily needs.

TURNING POINT

INTRODUCTION

Before we started Home Instead Senior Care, Paul worked for Merry Maids, the home-cleaning service. He learned a lot about the franchising world and the service industry through this remarkable company. It wasn't about cleaning toilets; it was about expanding a service company to meet the needs of its clients.

This was the foundation that prepared us for the moment we uncovered the glaring need for senior care. Some people think we were lucky to be the first in the industry to provide professional caregivers around the world the opportunity to care for seniors in their own homes, where most of them want to remain. We believe in the idea that luck is what happens when preparation meets opportunity. It has taken much planning and preparation to lay the foundation for this successful company.

In the same way, May was prepared to meet the opportunity that arose to care for her mother-in-law.

INSPIRATIONAL VERSE

This service that you perform is not only supplying the needs of God's people but is also overflowing in many expressions of thanks to God.

2 CORINTHIANS 9:12

MESSAGE

The Korean culture is strongly influenced by the teachings of Confucius. Those who are familiar with Confucianism may know that the one thing that is most emphasized is filial piety, the responsibility to take care of one's parents. In my generation it was thought disrespectful to search for outside help when caring for parents. It is natural for the children to be the main caregivers at all times. This does not really apply to the next generation, since more women are working.

Caring is defined as making provision and showing compassion. This makes sense only when the care recipient is either relatively weaker or at least willing to get help from others. The provider can do the best job when he or she is fully convinced that the recipient actually needs care, because compassion often is the best motivation for caregiving. Unfortunately, my in-laws did not fall under either category: they were neither weak nor willing to accept help.

When I got married, we decided to live with my in-laws in a house big enough for all of us. I naturally became their main caregiver, even though they did not really need help to live an independent life. Their health was far better than that of others, despite the aging process.

One winter my mother-in-law was hospitalized with a bad flu. As expected, all the family members took turns visiting her. When it was my turn, I found it almost unbelievable that she admitted she needed help from others now that she had become physically weaker. I was more than willing to provide care, the real care coming from compassion with love.

When she wanted to take a shower, I was there to become her supporting arms and legs. I was happy that I could help her wash her hair and her body. After her shower, I would hand-wash her undergarments, and again I was happy that I could do this for her. She didn't seem to mind, whereas she wouldn't have let me do this if she were not sick.

Although she was hospitalized for only a few days, that very week was a turning point for our relationship. My mother-in-law happily accepted my help when necessary. Caring for loved ones is definitely not an easy job. In my case, consistently approaching her regardless of her reaction was the key to successful caregiving.

Fortunately, even in her late eighties, my mother-in-law is still in fair health and remains at home. I now live in a separate house next door. I still gladly do the grocery shopping, run errands, and escort her to Sunday morning services as her caregiver and her companion.

May Park

"In my case, consistently approaching her regardless of her reaction was the key to successful caregiving."

CAREGIVER'S PRAYER

Jesus, my Friend,

You direct my steps and guide my decisions. Thank you for enhancing my relationship with my loved one. Help me to be patient and understanding, to be respectful of her wishes, and to be available. Lord, give me a servant's heart.

DEPTHS OF DEPRESSION

INTRODUCTION

I never want to go back to that time and place ever again; it was so dark and lonely. I had a brief bout of depression when the children were very young and Paul traveled a lot for business. It wasn't severe, but it warranted a few sessions with a counselor. I remember the heavy feeling of Satan having his hold on me, and I could not escape, my heart was filled with such sadness. It wasn't until my friend Terri started sharing her faith and what she had been learning through the Bible that I began to turn my focus away from myself and onto the Lord. I started studying the Bible with such a thirst and hunger for God's Word that it broke the chains of bondage I was feeling. I am forever grateful to God for delivering the Gospel of Salvation through my friend Terri that day. There is freedom and healing in God's Word.

Depression can occur at any age and at any stage of life. God guided Marian's father out of the darkness and back into the light.

INSPIRATIONAL VERSE

"When you are in distress and all these things have happened to you, then in later days you will return to the Lord your God and obey him. For the Lord your God is a merciful God; he will not abandon or destroy you or forget the covenant with your forefathers, which he confirmed to them by oath."

DEUTERONOMY 4:30–31

MESSAGE

It's still difficult to talk about my mother's death, not only because I miss her but also because of the impact her death had on our family. Her absence and the subsequent caregiving needs of my father exposed our family's strengths and weaknesses. When a family is shaken to its core, cracks sometimes develop more quickly than they can be repaired. The damage trickles down to other relationships, but love also trickles down, making forgiveness and hope possible.

Mom had Parkinson's disease, and I prayed that the Good Lord would take her before her symptoms became too painful for her. Instead, she was diagnosed with an aggressive form of lung cancer. I remember asking God: "What are you thinking?" My prayer had been answered. He did take her before her Parkinson's took control. She was given three months to live, but always one to get things done, she passed away one week short of three months.

Perhaps the cancer was meant to help us prepare for Mom's death. However, we could not have been ready for what happened next. She and our father had been married fifty-six years and had immigrated to America together. His wife's death was the first family death our dad had ever experienced. As with most couples, what happens to one partner's health seriously affects the other's. None of us were prepared for the fallout a mere two weeks later.

Without Mom, Dad fell into a deep depression that lasted over three years and eventually manifested as a severe psychological condition. After a suicide threat, he was involuntarily admitted for a mental health evaluation. While he was under evaluation, my six sisters and I discovered that Dad's affairs were not in order. He begged me to take him home, but we had bigger problems than getting him out of the hospital. We moved quickly to get his affairs in order. Dad's illness was difficult to manage and caused a strain among the seven sisters and our families.

Like that of many seniors, Dad's depression was not often discussed and not easily remedied. Although it was clear to everyone that he was clinically depressed, he was still a tough Irishman who was not going to accept the fact that he needed psychological help. Dad had always been such a positive person. I told him that I missed the man who, if one arm had been cut off, would say, "It's okay, I have another." Losing his beloved wife was like losing an arm. I reminded him he had another and a family who wanted him back.

Dad was able to find the will to live again. He got

on the right medications and slowly began to accept Mom's death. His grieving process was long, but he has been able to let go, for now, knowing full well that he will see her again someday. My parents had great faith, and that faith in action as Dad fought his way out from the depths of depression was a testament to God's love.

Dad's experience taught us all how deeply depression affects not only the person suffering from it but those who care for that person. My anxiety spilled into other areas of my life. When someone you love is terminally ill, or spiraling downward like my father, every little event begins to take priority even when it shouldn't. It's a fine line between caring for the dying and the ill and managing to care for the living and the well. I wasn't always successful in walking that line, and I've accepted responsibility for the damage my mistakes caused.

When Mom was sick, my sisters and I rotated care duties weekly. I was on duty the week of our parents' fifty-sixth wedding anniversary, when Mom was terminal. Knowing it would be their last anniversary, I prepared a special dinner and a small cake with candles. I set the table with Mom's linens and dishes from Ireland and placed their wedding photo as the centerpiece. This quiet celebration of a life together now serves as a gentle reminder to keep my marriage, children, and God as the centerpiece of my life. I am comforted knowing that, as long as I do, His love will continue to heal our wounds and strengthen the foundation of this family once again.

Marian Battersby

"It's a fine line between caring
for the dying and the ill and
managing to care for the living
and the well."

CAREGIVER'S PRAYER

Heavenly Counselor,

My heart is so grieved over the loss of my loved one, at times it feels unbearable. Give me strength and energy to move past these feelings of sadness and turn my gaze to you, O Lord. Fill my mind with the promises of your Word, for your Word stands firm and is unchanging. Give my soul peace and harmony in the knowledge that you will never fail me or abandon me.

BROTHERLY PEACE

INTRODUCTION

The similarities and differences among siblings have always fascinated me. My husband, Paul, comes from a big family, and while he and his siblings share family characteristics, each has a distinct personality. The six-year difference between my brother Mark and me meant we had less time together when we were children. But as adults we share many of the same challenges of marriage and children. My sister and I share similar beliefs and have a close relationship but are very different women. I see something similar in the dynamics among our four children. They were all raised in exactly the same environment, yet each has grown to be his or her own person, with unique opinions, dreams, and views on the world.

The differences between Dana and his brother caused them to drift apart and become estranged. Dana willingly shares his story of their family's struggle to make brotherly peace.

MESSAGE

Stubbornness, pride, and some good old-fashioned male ego kept my brother, Rick, and me from speaking for many years. Being estranged from your only brother, or any family member, isn't for the fainthearted. Let me tell you, it requires enormous dedication to reach the level of foolishness that we attained!

Unfortunately, during the time of our estrangement, our elderly mother's dementia was rapidly worsening. Our mother was far wiser than her two thickheaded sons and many years ago had purchased a long-term care insurance policy. Smartest thing she could have done! The financial part of her care is covered, and not having to worry about that has been an absolute blessing. The policy includes in-home care, so she receives one-on-one attention in the Florida condo she loves.

It is difficult being away from Mom, but keeping her in the home she loves is the best option. Over the years my brother and I have both made frequent trips to care for her. Never together, mind you; he did his thing for her and I did mine. Working together and being logical is not part of the deal when you've firmly committed yourself not to speak to your only brother.

All kidding aside, being estranged from family

members isn't natural. Even as a grown man, I felt incomplete without my brother in my life. Rick and I are both family guys, and our wives and kids are the best things that ever happened to either of us. Family is the most important thing, and when I think about the years that Rick and I didn't include each other in that equation, I feel ashamed. Not only did we not put the needs of our mother ahead of our own foolish pride but we set a terrible example for the kids we both love so much. Fortunately, those days are behind us now.

What tore us apart is also what ultimately brought us back together: the care of our mother. I had tried unsuccessfully to reach Mom on New Year's Eve and was worried. My brother called the next day to tell me that she had fallen and was in the hospital. That call was not warm by any means, but it was just enough to break the ice.

Shortly after that, we ran into each other at a basketball game at Madison Square Garden in New York City. Nineteen thousand fans, and the two people we run into? Rick and his son! There is no convincing me that God wasn't guiding us through that crowd. We all shook hands, hugged, and talked about the game, which was our first conversation about anything other than Mom. After that we continued to talk and check in with each other. During that time my eldest son became engaged to his college sweetheart. My first call was to Rick to share the news. The wedding invitations went out, and my brother was very happy to RSVP, saying, "We wouldn't miss it!"

Seeing my brother and his family walk into the

lobby at the wedding was one of my life's unforgettable moments. We hugged and both cried as he said to me, "You are my big brother, and we are all that we have left." Right there and then, surrounded by our wonderful families, we set the right example. On a day devoted to love and family, we reconciled as brothers.

We both wished Mom could have attended the wedding. But she was too weak to travel and her dementia was too far advanced. She is no longer aware enough to know that we are speaking again. I hope she has also forgotten that we had ever stopped.

Mom's care is stronger now because it is being administered by a combined love and unified family. Our top priority is keeping her comfortable. It turns out, we make our best decisions together, and caregiving is easier when we work as partners. We are in it together. Even though Mom isn't aware that we have each other again, I know it would make her extremely happy.

Dana Goodman

"What tore us apart is also what ultimately brought us back together."

CAREGIVER'S PRAYER

Elohim,

You are the God of the past, present, and future. You know our hearts and our intentions. Help me to put the needs of my loved one ahead of my own foolish pride. Help me to work through conflicts with family members with dignity and respect, and let me set a strong example for my children. Lord, you are "merciful and gracious, slow to anger and abounding in steadfast love."

BLISSFULLY UNAWARE

INTRODUCTION

A flyer was sent around the grade school announcing an outbreak of lice. My son, Marty, was scratching his head frequently. I feared he had become infested with the tiny beasts but hoped I was just being paranoid. I had a dream that night urging me to check his head. Sure enough, he had lice! I was mortified! How long had we been unaware that these little critters were present on a few of us?

We immediately found the right remedies and started treatments. The kids remained blissfully unaware that there was anything to worry about. They were having a ball as Paul and I slapped mayonnaise on all our heads and covered them with shower caps. Boy, were we a mayonnaise mess! There was no sense crying about it, so we laughed and made the most of it. Lice outbreaks are something most people would want to forget about immediately, but this has become a family memory that the six of us will never forget. We even took pictures to commemorate this unusual event.

Whether it's lice or cancer, it's not what happens to us that matters; it's how we react to the situation that truly defines us.

This family chose their blessings over their anger, and time together over household chores. Putting one another first is an honorable aim for any family.

INSPIRATIONAL VERSE

Now faith is being sure of what we hope for and certain of what we do not see. . . . And without faith it is impossible to please God, because anyone who comes to him must believe that he exists and that he rewards those who earnestly seek him.

HEBREWS 11:1, 6

MESSAGE

In early 2005, my mother was unexpectedly diagnosed with terminal lung cancer, which changed everything. Our family was in a crisis that no one expected. Mom was sixty-seven, and Dad was seventy-two, still young by today's standards.

My mother was very far into the disease before it was found, and her condition deteriorated rapidly. Because she always had thorough yearly checkups, it was difficult for the nurse in me to accept that this had come on so suddenly. Additional research uncovered a spot, which had been missed on an X-ray eighteen months before. At first we were angry and briefly considered legal action, but we knew that wasn't the solution. Eventually we embraced that unrevealed diagnosis as a blessing. Rather than spending the last eighteen months of her life fighting an uphill battle, my mother lived fully, perhaps blissfully unaware of the cancer cells within her body.

My father had his own health issues and was able to provide only minimal assistance to my mother. As an RN, I wondered how I could have not recognized the decline in my father's abilities. How is it that I am able to see so clearly the signs of denial in the families I work with but couldn't see that I was experiencing the same thing within my own family?

Initially, my parents were reluctant to accept the help they needed to stay at home. Our roles were reversed. I was parenting the parents, and it was a challenge to get my parents on board with a plan. I am so grateful that we decided to bring in professional help. The home care services allowed my sister and me to spend the last few months of Mom's life as her daughters rather than worrying about chores and tasks.

Mom had been abundantly generous with her time and had given us the gift of a wonderful childhood; we wanted to make her final months just as special. My sister and I moved back to our family home, and for a short period, it felt like we were children again, back home as a family. When I reflect on those final months with Mom, I feel overjoyed that we were able to be truly present with her during those last days to pray, talk, and laugh. I will be forever grateful that we were there to see her last smile.

After our mother passed, my sister and I discovered

the full extent of Dad's inability to care for himself. We wanted to continue with home care, but my father weighs in excess of 330 pounds and could not move about safely. The family home, with small bathrooms and narrow doorways, could not accommodate the equipment needed for his care. He was noncompliant with his medications and diet, even with caregivers in the home. Ultimately, Dad agreed to assisted living, but that quickly progressed to personal care. Now Dad resides in skilled nursing care.

Anyone who thinks placing a loved one in a facility means less work is mistaken. I am still his caregiver. Visiting at the nursing home, managing his finances, dealing with doctors' appointments and follow-up care, paying bills, sorting mail, shopping, et cetera, is equivalent to a part-time job. When you love someone, you don't mind the responsibility, but it doesn't erase the guilt over not being able to keep your loved one at home.

Dad now has dementia. Like Mom, he is also unaware of the changes in his health. I often wish that we could take him home, be his little girls again, and surround him with love, as we were able to do with Mom. It is in those moments that I remind myself I cannot control what happens next; I can only control how I react to my situations. I know, in God's hands, everything will work out the way it was meant to be.

Colette Hofelich

"When I reflect on those final months with Mom, I feel overjoyed that we were able to be truly present with her during those last days to pray, talk, and laugh."

CAREGIVER'S PRAYER

Holy, Holy Lord,

Illuminate my mind to understand your will for me and help me earnestly seek you with all my heart. Let me put my faith and trust in you, Lord, to make me aware of the right solutions for my parents' care so that I may rest peacefully. Our struggles are small compared with the great God we serve.

NO HOPE?

INTRODUCTION

When I was in ninth grade, our youth group invited three other churches to join us for a fall retreat at Camp Hitchcock. What a glorious experience that was— singing songs of praise, worshiping God out in nature, and meeting new friends who had hearts for the Lord. It was there that I accepted Jesus Christ as my personal savior. I learned at that retreat that nothing could separate me from the love of God that is in Jesus Christ, neither death nor life, neither angels nor demons, nor anything else in all creation. This message of God's love gives me great hope.

Georgene clings to her faith but doesn't give up hope as she gives her dying mother permission to let go.

INSPIRATIONAL VERSE

Let us hold unswervingly to the hope we pro-
fess, for he who promised is faithful.

HEBREWS 10:23

MESSAGE

No hope. That was the report from one doctor after another. But how could that be? Just a month before Mom
was fine. Or so it seemed. We knew she hadn't been feeling well. But one doctor visit and test after another failed
to reveal a serious problem.

That is until Dad called one early August night to report that Mom, seventy-seven, was in a hospital sixty
miles from my hometown. "Nothing to worry about," he
said. "Just a minor stroke, but they are keeping her for
observation." I drove there just in time to get the news
that would begin our family's journey down that slippery
slope of no return.

More tests had revealed an aggressive and rare form
of uterine cancer, which had gone undiagnosed. Bad
news seemed to mount. Mom's CAT scan looked like a
thunderstorm brewing on a midwestern summer's night.
A major stroke was imminent. Treating the stroke risk
would likely make her bleeding from the cancer worse.

We were racing against the clock, and Mom knew it.
She had become sullen and withdrawn. That's when
the guilt began to engulf me. Mom had been sick at
least a year. I was the daughter, the oldest. I should have
known how sick she was. I should have done more.

What's worse, I worked in the senior care industry as a writer. I conveyed plenty of advice from experts about how family caregivers should take care of their aging parents. It seemed that I couldn't even take care of my own mom.

We drove Mom to our home, where we made an appointment at a prominent cancer center. The oncology surgeon assigned to her case was a compassionate woman who assured us that she would move swiftly. Surgery was scheduled in five days. Back home Mom seemed weak and ill. A day after she'd arrived at our house, she began coughing up blood.

We rushed her back to the hospital, where she would await surgery. When we bade her good-bye that Saturday night, it was the last conversation we would ever have with Mom. The phone call that awakened us at four in the morning was from a nurse with the devastating news. The massive stroke doctors feared had happened. Finding Mom in a coma in the wee hours of the morning was horrific. Dad nearly collapsed from that sight.

The next few days were a blur. One afternoon the oncology doctor asked us to gather at Mom's bedside. She was the first of several doctors to utter those heart-piercing words: "I'm sorry. There is nothing more we can do," she explained. "There's no hope, no brain activity, no way to change the outcome." We cried, and the doctor fought back tears as well.

I began to feel uncomfortable, wishing that we weren't having this exchange in front of Mom. I'd heard stories about people in comas who could hear everything going on around them. What if Mom was listening to her own death sentence? The professionals kept saying she couldn't hear us, but I wasn't so sure.

I wanted to have just one more talk with her. I needed to know that Mom was okay. She'd always had a strong faith, having accepted Christ at a summer camp when she was sixteen. For years she'd coordinated funeral and church dinners, baked her Czech delicacies for special occasions, and made sure her family lived their faith.

But I knew Mom would be worried about leaving us, saying good-bye to me and my brother; her grandchildren, who were only seven, eight, and nine years old; and her sweetheart of fifty-three years, my dad.

The next day I found myself alone by her bedside. I thought I would give it a try. "You know, Mom, we'll be fine," I said. "Dad will always love you. You don't need to be afraid of anything. You know where you're going. You can go in peace." I glanced over at her, and that's when I noticed it—a small tear trickling out the corner of her eye. The realization that my message may have been heard was overwhelming.

A few days later, an ambulance transported Mom to the town of her birth, where she had lived all but a few years of her life. For the next two weeks, longtime friends and family made the trek to her hospital bed to share their memories and say good-bye. I think she heard every one of them. Mom died September 3, 2001, with my dad at her bedside. After she had been in a coma for three weeks, Dad said she opened her eyes for one last look at him before she passed on.

No hope? It's a prognosis I'll never accept.

Georgene Lahm

"For the next two weeks, longtime friends and family made the trek to her hospital bed to share their memories and say good-bye."

CAREGIVER'S PRAYER

God of Hope and Peace,

What would I do without my faith in you, Lord? I would be lost. Thank you for giving me hope to push on with my mother's care and treatments. I am grateful that I could be there for her in her last days to care for and comfort her as she transitioned from this life to eternity.

LIFELONG FRIEND

INTRODUCTION

Our son, Marty, enjoyed playing baseball when he was younger, mainly because of the wonderful coaches who took an interest in him off the field as well as on. They taught him sportsmanship and the importance of being a good team player. These coaches invested a lot of time and energy with our son to improve his game. Marty held these gentlemen in high regard then and continues to have special relationships with them now. Mentors like these can really make a difference in the life of a child. Don't we pray for good men to come alongside our sons to encourage, support, and enhance the lessons we have taught them?

Dan is the man he is today because of the role a mentor played in his life.

INSPIRATIONAL VERSE

"My command is this: Love each other as I have loved you. Greater love has no one than this, that one lay down his life for his friends."

JOHN 15:12–13

MESSAGE

Since 1950 Rosenblatt Stadium in Omaha has been known as the home of the Men's College World Series. As a typical American boy, I loved everything about the game of baseball and spent as much time as I was allowed at the fields. When I was twelve, I started my first "job" as a ball boy for the Omaha Royals, our hometown minor league team. And let me tell you, for a kid from Omaha, life didn't get any better than spending summer vacation at the ballpark!

It was there, in the dugouts and summer heat, that I met Paul, a scout for the Milwaukee Brewers. Hands down, he was the coolest guy I had ever met! Paul had been a second baseman for the Chicago Cubs and the New York Yankees for many years before becoming a coach and a scout. He knew everything there was to know about the game, and I hung out to "talk baseball" with him every chance I could.

Despite the difference in our age, an unlikely friendship developed between us that has become one of the most enduring friendships of my life. Who would ever have guessed that cool scout from Milwaukee and this kid from Omaha would still be talking baseball nearly forty years later? I used to tell Paul that he just got lucky I had room in my otherwise packed schedule to spend time with him. To which he'd toss back some remark about it being me who got lucky. In the end, I don't believe luck had anything at all to do with our meeting. We both did a lot of praying during those games, and as it is often said, God sometimes answers our prayers in a way that's better than we know how to ask.

Paul is a decorated World War II veteran and truly proud to be an American. His stories about battlefields, brotherhood, and serving our country have been a constant source of inspiration for me. The lessons I've learned about being a man through his stories about duty, honor, and pride cannot be found in books. Nor can the lessons I've learned from him about loyalty and friendship.

Paul is now eighty-four years old, and people often assume I am his son. He usually has some clever retort about how he is far too good-looking, smart, or funny to be my dad. When I was younger, and even sometimes now, my friends would wonder why I hang out with this old guy if I don't have to. "If he's not your relative, why do you *have* to help care for him?" What they don't understand is that I *get* to help care for Paul, which I consider a great honor.

One of my favorite memories with Paul happened shortly after his last surviving brother, John, died. The two of them had grown up in the heart of Mark Twain's America and returned to their hometown of Hannibal, Missouri, to share a home after retirement. So after John died, whether Paul would admit it or not, he was lonely. I decided to go spend a weekend with him, and we stayed busy doing odds and ends around his place. After our "chores" were done, he seemed unusually quiet. I assumed he was tired from the busy day.

I was heading home first thing in the morning. Before I left that evening, I asked him if there was anything else I could do for him. He didn't say anything for a long time, but finally he said, "Sit down and be quiet." I am certain he had said those same words to me many times during games at good old Rosenblatt Stadium, but this time, I did as I was instructed.

After several more minutes of silence, he said, "Since John died, I don't have anyone to sit and watch the games with, so will you stay and watch the game with me?" John's favorite team, the St. Louis Cardinals, was playing, and I'll never forget watching the game with Paul that night.

On my way back to the hotel after the game, I was struck with how our perspective on what's important changes as we grow older. Paul didn't care about the chores we had done that day or the conversations we'd had about his future. All he really wanted was to have someone to watch the game with him. I was so happy I could be there to do just that.

Paul didn't have children of his own, so maybe that's why God introduced us when he did. As unlikely as it may seem, that twelve-year-old kid and the cool baseball scout have made a good team over the years. He has always been there for me, and now that he's the coolest guy in the nursing home, I'm still there for him. Paul's mind is as sharp as a tack and he's as feisty as ever, so he really doesn't need much. Knowing that he still has a trusted buddy who will always have his back is enough for him.

I help Paul with decisions about his care, but what he really needs from me is what he has always had, my friendship. So now when I visit, I remind myself "to sit down and be quiet" and not get so busy taking care of him that I forget to care about him.

Dan Wieberg

"*God sometimes answers our prayers in a way that's better than we know how to ask.*"

CAREGIVER'S PRAYER
Dear Heavenly One,

Help me to sit and be still in your presence and meditate on your goodness. Thank you for blessing my life with unique friendships. I have gleaned much wisdom and perspective from my caregiving encounters. I am filled with joy and gratitude that you have allowed me to make a difference in someone else's life.

DO IT NOW

INTRODUCTION

I hate to admit this, but I am a recovering procrastinator. All my life I have battled this condition, and now I am trying to overcome it by practicing the opposite: proactivity. In Mary Kay Cosmetics, we were trained to be part of the DIN, DIN Club. Do It Now, Do It Now. I would make signs and hang them on my bathroom mirror, on my refrigerator, and in my car to remind me to "Do It Now" instead of later. For instance, when God tells me to call a friend who has been on my mind, or write someone an encouraging note, Do It Now, because God may want to use me as His vehicle to touch another person's life in a special way.

Franny does not procrastinate. She is bold in providing care for her mother.

INSPIRATIONAL VERSE

For God did not give us a spirit of timidity, but a spirit of power, of love and of self-discipline.

2 TIMOTHY 1:7

MESSAGE

I have been a registered nurse for twenty-nine years and have cared for people of all ages in hospital, home-care, and school settings. I have educated patients, caregivers, and family members about how to care for themselves and loved ones, and have taught nursing students in clinical settings. It is what I always wanted to do. I continue to manage our seniors' care now while they age in place through nonmedical home care. It all came so easily to me until my own mother was diagnosed with metastatic colon cancer. As much as I continued to assess and plan for my mother's care, I immediately became the caregiver. In addition, although I had two brothers in the area, I was the only caregiver available to meet the needs of my parents.

When Mom returned from Florida last January for a temporary stay at home, she began to describe some problems she had been having, and they were all symptoms of cancer. I immediately started a calendar of appointments, keeping my brothers and family informed of weekly progress. My father was best left in Florida because of his health until the final diagnosis was determined. It was then that I called my brother and told him, "Mom is going to find out next week that she has cancer, so you need to go to Florida and bring Dad home." The following week, with family gathered at the hospital, she had surgery and, after recovery, started the first round of chemotherapy.

I couldn't put the stress of Mom's doctors' appointments, chemo visits, tests, and referrals solely on the shoulders of my eighty-three-year-old father. We split up the duties and became Mom's personal team of caregivers. My father cared for himself and Mom as she recovered from surgery and rested after rounds of chemotherapy. I assumed the role of my mother's advocate and handled all appointments and communications with her doctors and the family.

This year certainly strengthened my relationship with my parents, but it wasn't ever about seeing them for pleasure anymore. The amount of information that is given to an oncology patient between tests, chemo treatments, ER visits, and the required referrals and insurance approvals is overwhelming. As a health care professional, I often wonder how seniors can be expected to understand and handle this on their own.

It has been a sad year, watching my mom, a once vibrant and fast-paced woman, age before my eyes. She had regularly visited her primary doctor, and they were always watchful for signs of diabetes because her mother and two sisters had been diagnosed with that disease. Too bad the doctor never told her about the need for a routine colonoscopy. The year ended with Mom resting in Florida until she needed to come home for her last test, which, we hoped, would bring the good news that surgery could remove those tumors from her liver.

The tumors, it turned out, could be removed, but there was a shadow on the duct of the pancreas, and we had to rule out further cancer. I left the office and was immediately on the phone with Mom's primary physician to get a referral for an MRI and then to schedule the MRI and call yet another surgeon's office for an appointment. It felt like a never-ending road, and Mom and I were both praying for a rest stop!

While we were at the hospital for her MRI, I had to go feed the parking meter. After leaving my mother alone, I went out and found a ticket on my windshield. *I lost it!* For the first time in a long time, there on the streets of Philly, I had just had it! Realizing that this year was starting the same as last year was more than I could handle in that moment.

So here we go again—more appointments, scheduled surgery, surgery canceled because of an ice storm, more unnecessary stress for Mom, surgery rescheduled, and finally some good news—the tumor looked cancer-free!

Mom went off to recovery in ICU, where with older patients comes an added problem. Narcotics and anesthesia for the elderly coupled with the sleep deprivation inevitable in ICU are a recipe for disaster. It's called ICU psychosis; a pleasantly confused individual becomes agitated and combative. Let's throw in a few more drugs to agitate a woman who just lost half of her liver. As a nurse I expected this, but being a daughter who is watching her mother behave like somebody she's not was surreal. I feel for families who are just learning about such things.

Every time I told Mom that she was fine, it seemed that something else would happen so she began to think I was hiding things from her, and sometimes, I do. She told me she didn't need my help anymore, that she and Dad could take care of everything. It took a little tough love and my saying, "Okay, Ma, have it your way," and stepping away to make her stop pushing me away. We had a heart-to-heart. I told Mom she had two choices: be angry and unhappy or accept the fact that she has cancer and live with it! She chose acceptance.

Brighter days appear to be ahead. Mom is on the road to recovery, and I've just realized how exhausted I am. Owning my own business and having a terrific husband to keep it running have been a godsend. Once I get Mom back to Florida, it's time to take care of Franny. The gym . . . a colonoscopy . . . It will come.

Franny Fox

> "I told Mom she had two choices: be angry and unhappy or accept the fact that she has cancer and live with it! She chose acceptance."

CAREGIVER'S PRAYER

Jesus, Our Great Advocate,

This caregiving situation has really tested my patience. Help me to advocate for my parents and be proactive in getting the best care and treatments for them. Thank you for giving me a bold spirit and the stamina I need to carry on day after day. You are the Rock on which I lean.

MY HIGHEST PRIVILEGE

INTRODUCTION

I remember when I was nineteen years old, my family stood by my grandfather's bedside in the hospital as he took his very last breath. I had never seen anyone die before. I didn't know what to expect. The nurse rushed to the window to open it and explained that she believed the soul needed a way to escape to heaven. I was actually waiting for the moment that Jesus would appear in the room and take my grandfather's soul to heaven. Of course that didn't visibly happen, but in the spiritual realm I believe it did. I felt privileged to witness something so sacred—the very last breath of life, as did Tami, in the following story.

INSPIRATIONAL VERSE

I have set the Lord always before me.
Because he is my right hand,
I will not be shaken.

Therefore my heart is glad and my tongue re-
　　joices;
my body also will rest secure,
because you will not abandon me to the
　　grave,
nor will you let your Holy One see decay.
You have made known to me the path of life;
you will fill me with joy in your presence,
with eternal pleasures at your right hand.

PSALM 16:8–11

MESSAGE

It is through reflection that I am humbled to know that
I am a part of God's extraordinary plan. It is only in
retrospect that we are able to appreciate how sometimes seemingly unrelated circumstances trigger a series of events that could be attributed only to our
gracious Savior, Lord Jesus Christ. Blessed are we who
listen to our instincts and allow our hearts to guide us.
This is indeed how our Lord speaks. For whoever needs
to hear His voice, may their ears be opened.

That's how it happened last July 2. Plans that I had
been really excited about for the holiday suddenly collapsed early that Friday afternoon. However, our Lord
had other plans for me that evening, and it was a divine appointment I gladly accepted. One of my highest
privileges is when I know I am being used by God to
help others.

I work part-time as a professional caregiver for the

elderly, so it is not uncommon for me to get called for an extra assignment here and there. Jessi works for Home Instead Senior Care. I knew if she was calling, it must be something important.

Jessi had just taken a call from a woman who desperately needed respite during her mother's final stages of life. Jessi knew I normally did not take overnights because of my full-time job, but she said the name Tami instantly came to her, so she took a chance that I might be available.

I can't explain it, but I felt compelled to be there for this client, even though I had never met either the mother, Alice, or the daughter, Nicole. Nicole, an only child, had been by her mother's bedside for over a week. She had said her good-byes multiple times. Any breath could have been Alice's last. Having had previous hospice experience, I recognized how emotionally drained and physically exhausted Nicole was.

It takes enormous courage to step away from the bedside of a dying parent, and I was very sensitive to that when I spoke with Nicole. I asked if she would tell me about her mother so I could know what she had been like. I assured her that Alice would not be alone, and that gave Nicole peace to leave for the night.

I then stepped aside as Nicole walked to her mother's bedside and prayed. She whispered that it was okay and that Jesus was waiting for her. It was at that moment that I knew it was not just by chance that I was here. The Lord had guided me, knowing that I shared a deep faith connection with Alice and Nicole. This knowledge opened up the opportunity for me to speak with Alice in a language she would recognize and appreciate.

The door closed and I sat quietly for a few minutes, just feeling Alice's presence in the room. I vividly remember thinking, I need to get busy, and quickly introduced myself to her. I sat by her side and stroked her hand as I spoke about surrendering and releasing herself fully to Christ. The words of a hymn that I had known as a child came to mind, and I began to sing:

> *Fairest Lord Jesus, Ruler of all nature,*
> *O Thou of God and man the Son;*
> *Thee will I cherish, Thee will I honor,*
> *Thou, my soul's glory, joy, and crown.*

On Alice's nightstand was a devotional with a worn cover and tattered pages. I noticed many dog-eared corners and underlined sentences that must have had special meaning for her. For the next hour or so, I read each of those well-loved pages aloud as I continued to touch her hand.

The room filled with a joyous energy, and I told Alice that she had a party to go to and a better place to be. I straightened her sheets and brushed her silver hair. I felt as though I was dressing Cinderella for the gala ball. It was so easy to be cheerful as I spoke about what a glorious gathering it would be.

I had mentally prepared myself for a long night and possibly a long weekend. I decided it was time to change into some comfy clothes. As I gathered my bag, I kept chatting with Alice about what a great night we were going to have, singing, praying, and reading more from her beloved devotional.

Just as I turned to walk away, the raspy breathing that had filled the quiet space stopped. Her chest lifted slightly as she took a sip of air and then gently collapsed on that final exhale. She was gone, and it took my breath away. I did not go to her immediately. I stayed back to let Alice have this very private moment with God. My tears were not because I had known her a long time but out of pure joy that she had discovered the strength to continue her journey. I think I was there not for receiving but rather for giving energy. I was able to offer a hand as Alice took her first step to cross the bridge.

I stayed with her as the hospice nurses lovingly prepared her body for its next stage. I stayed not because I was being paid to do so but in honor of her daughter, who was strong enough to let go so that Alice could do the same. I stayed because Nicole had put Alice's care in my hands, but I was merely a conduit as Jesus took her hand from mine.

Several weeks later Jessi forwarded me a letter from Nicole, thanking me for all I had done that night. I feel so grateful that I answered God's call and didn't allow the noise of a spoiled holiday to lead me elsewhere. I am indeed honored and privileged by this experience. I sit in awe of His almighty powers that connected Jessi, Nicole, and me to Alice forevermore.

Tami Hillyer

*"One of my highest privileges
is when I know I am being used
by God to help others."*

CAREGIVER'S PRAYER

Fairest Lord Jesus,

You use us in many ways for your holy purposes. Thank you for allowing me to witness to others the Gospel of our Lord Jesus in their lives and in their time of death. It is an honor to care for someone right up till the very last breath. My highest privilege is when I know that I am being used in a special way, by you, God, to help others.

LIVING IN GRATITUDE

INTRODUCTION

Our family vacations take us to the Colorado mountains several times a year. Whenever we are high up on a ski lift breathing in that brisk mountain air or hiking through a brilliant green valley sprinkled with colorful wildflowers, we always stop and say, "This is God's country." We see the "purple mountain majesties" and marvel at God's attention to detail in everything He has created. We are so blessed by God's earthly beauty. Much of the time we do not have to travel far to see that beauty; it is in our own backyards. God wants us to express our gratitude for the beautiful things in our lives that give us joy to see, touch, and smell.

Brad declares his grateful heart for the many blessings that God has bestowed upon his family and his mother's health.

INSPIRATIONAL VERSE
You are my God, and I will give you thanks;
you are my God, and I will exalt you.
Give thanks to the Lord, for he is good;
his love endures forever.

PSALM 118:28–29

MESSAGE

I have always felt grateful for the wonderful life I have lived. I feel blessed that an amazing woman agreed to marry me, and together we have built a charmed life: beautiful children, successful careers, a nice home, and good relationships with our family, friends, and church.

However, in the last few years, I have learned the difference between feeling grateful in response to life and practicing a life of gratitude. Gratitude allows you to be the best you can be and encourages others to do the same. For me, starting each day from a state of gratitude is humbling and keeps me closer to God than I have ever been.

What caused this shift in my perception? After years of service, traveling around the world, spending time away from my family, I realized that my big corporate job with its great perks was no longer fulfilling. The thought of continuing this rat race became more distasteful every day. My decision for change was only reaffirmed when I was asked to relocate my family to Chicago. I felt compelled to slow down and consider all the possibilities of what my future, the future of family, could hold.

I would often call my mother, Gerry, for her business advice. She encouraged me to find something that I was passionate about. The support of my wife, my kids, and my mother reminded me that what I love the most is my family. So the question became, How could I make a career out of that?

Shortly after having that thought, I was presented with an opportunity to buy a business that provided nonmedical in-home care and companionship to seniors. Provide care for other families? Perfect! After all, my mother had lived next door for the past fifteen years, so I was nearly an expert on family caregiving. Or so I thought.

Yes, Mom does live next door to us, and we share backyards on the same acreage. Up until a few months ago, she was driving the tractor, mowing the grass, mulching hay, and so on. Hardly the definition of a senior who needed much caregiving, but I still felt like our experience with her since Dad died twenty years ago helped qualify me to run this business. Mom was very involved as we took over the business. I was thankful to have her as my sounding board.

It was December 6 of last year when I received the call from my mother. In her slurred speech, she indicated that she believed she was having a stroke and needed to get to a hospital. My time in the business had re-educated me about the warning signs, and with the assistance of my RN I immediately dialed 911 and raced home. In fact, Mom's awareness may have saved her life and certainly lessened the damage. We got to the hospital quickly enough for her to be given TPA (tissue plasminogen activator), a "clot-buster" that is often referred to as the miracle drug for stroke victims.

Although she was given this miracle drug, I ran through the normal emotions of wondering if Mom would recover or if she would die. But then I realized I knew exactly what needed to be done. We needed to get her into a rehabilitation facility and get her home, where she stood the best chance for full recovery. I thought, If I had still been working at my old job, I wouldn't have known what to do. I would have gone into a state of crisis and just been grateful for whatever help anyone could offer.

And wow, did we get all the help we needed and more! The caregivers who had gotten to know Mom through the business were lining up to be part of her caregiving team once she came home from rehab. By this time, I had owned the business for a little over a year and thought I had a deep appreciation for the services our caregivers provide to seniors. Wrong again! These professionals fought their way to our acreage through one of the worst snowstorms to work their shifts. They came in on holidays as we needed them. The dedication of these professional caregivers is nothing short of miraculous.

Mom is on the road to recovery and was recently telling me that she is eager to return to her job as honorary senior services director. As she spoke with such excitement in her voice, I realized how blessed I was in the crossroads of my life to be there for Mom when she needed me most. I had been freed to follow the path that allowed me to know how to care for the person who had always been there to care for me. God put me on the path to serve others and had been preparing me to help my own mother when she needed me.

My life is so much larger and my heart more open than I could have ever imagined. *Grateful* doesn't begin to cover how I feel. It's more than a feeling; it is an energy that is fueled by giving without expectation of what you will get in return. Gratitude—as an action, a verb, and a strategy for life—produces amazing results.

Brad Snively

> *"I have learned the difference between feeling grateful in response to life and practicing a life of gratitude."*

CAREGIVER'S PRAYER

Beautiful Savior,

My heart is full of gratitude for the many blessings you have imparted to me: a wonderful family, a beautiful home, and meaningful work. Let me live out my gratitude in ways that are pleasing to you. You want us to have an abundant life and have it to the full. How great thou art!

GOD'S DOMINOES

INTRODUCTION

Paul and our youngest daughter, Jacquelyn, are daredevils on snowboards. They like to float through trees and down black diamond trails, giving high fives as they conquer each challenge. Until one run turned their total elation into total fear. Jacquelyn had fallen headfirst down a steep slope and torpedoed into a tree. Not knowing if she was dead or alive, Paul began to pray out of sheer desperation. Jacquelyn was so fortunate to incur only minor bruising to her shoulder and ribs, and, *yes,* a pounding headache that lasted for days. She realized that God had prevented serious injury and death. She knew He had spared her life, and that meant God had a greater purpose yet for her to fulfill.

We have all struggled to discern our greater purpose in life. Marge and Laura are no exceptions. Through their multiple family caregiving experiences, God led them to their meaningful new careers.

INSPIRATIONAL VERSE

And we know that in all things God works for the good of those who love him, who have been called according to his purpose.

ROMANS 8:28

MESSAGE

Caring for our mother, Helen Green, forever changed the course of our lives. Our caregiving journey led us to a new profession and the opportunity to build a business together that serves a greater purpose. As in a game of dominoes, the timing was perfect and everything fell into place. Our experience as second-generation family caregivers allowed us to become professional caregivers. We both wholeheartedly believe that God placed us exactly where we were meant to be, running an in-home senior care business for His glory.

When we opened the doors of our new business, we dedicated the office to our mother and to God, to remind us of the journey that brought us to this place.

Marge My caregiving experience began by having both my mother and my grandmother live with me and my children. Mom was taking care of Grandma in my home while I worked a full-time job and raised my children. After Grandma died, Mom began showing the signs of Parkinson's. I felt fortunate that she was already in my home, but having her live with me to care for Grandma was far different from my having to care for my mother around the clock.

Mom slowly became more and more forgetful. To say the least, the constant shifting between working, caring for her, and being present for my children was a strain. At this point, none of us knew that in-home care for seniors was even available. I did the best I could to manage her care with the support of my sisters and brothers.

My first big hurdle was being forced to take Mom's car and driver's license away. Not only is taking someone's sense of independence a difficult thing to do, but it also created the challenge of daily transportation for her. Arranging a bus service to take her to the store, appointments, and so on was added to my daily to-do list, which was growing at a pace that I could no longer keep up with.

I became so overwhelmed that I couldn't handle it anymore. I had to ask for help. I contacted my sister Laura Purcell in Massachusetts, and she and her family moved to Florida to help. Mom lived with Laura and her family for one year, and then we had to place her in a nursing home within five miles of her three daughters. Mom knew she needed more care and was ready to go into a facility, but we all still actively cared for her even after the move. One of us would see her every day, and one of us would be there every evening.

Shortly after the move, I lost my job because of the downturn in the economy. At this point, I just threw my hands in the air and asked God to direct me to where He needed me to be. During that period of moving Mom to the nursing home, Laura and I had looked at the opportunity to open a senior care franchise. Could this be the purposeful, meaningful work God wanted us to do?

Laura The toughest challenge for me was to accept that Mom could no longer care for herself. She was a college-educated career woman who had raised five children. She was always so independent that it was devastating to see her in that state. To watch her deteriorate and not be able to stop it was unbelievably frustrating. I felt relief when she passed because I know how horrible it must have been for her to live in her diminished condition.

Mom was committed to caring for her mother because she felt it was her God-given duty. We were fortunate to be able to keep Grandma at home until she passed away. Unfortunately, we were not able to keep our mother at home due to her illness. But we felt that same sense of duty and honor to care for Mom, regardless of whether she was at home or at the care facility. Little could we have known that the lessons we learned through caregiving would one day be used in a business that allows us to care for others.

I believe that the Lord led both Marge and me to this career, perhaps as a way to fill the void of caring for Mom but also to educate others about the options available for the elderly. And perhaps Marge and I are just two of God's dominoes, strategically placed where He needed us, to carry on a tradition of caregiving.

Marge Thompson and Laura Purcell

"*At this point, I just threw my hands in the air and asked God to take me to where He needed me to be.*"

CAREGIVER'S PRAYER

All-Powerful and All-Knowing Lord,

You always know what is best for me. When I feel overwhelmed or frustrated, I know I can turn to you for strength and assurance. Allow me to learn from my caregiving experiences so that I may continue to help others who may need companionship and assistance.

UNSPOKEN TRUTH

INTRODUCTION

When I was a beauty consultant with Mary Kay Cosmetics, my director, Cindy, would talk about the need for a "checkup from the neck up." What did she mean? She explained that we needed to examine our attitudes, to make sure we didn't have any negative thinking going on in our heads. We have the power to control our attitudes and can choose to have a positive attitude instead of letting negative thoughts take over and determine our actions or reactions.

Martha Washington once said, "I've learned from experience that the greater part of our happiness or misery depends on our dispositions and not on our circumstances." There again, it's all about our attitude.

The writer of this message struggles to share her strong feelings about her undesired position as a caregiver.

INSPIRATIONAL VERSE

Finally, brothers, whatever is true, whatever is noble, whatever is right, whatever is pure, whatever is lovely, whatever is admirable—if anything is excellent or praiseworthy—think about such things. Whatever you have learned or received or heard from me, or seen in me—put it into practice. And the God of peace will be with you.

PHILIPPIANS 4:8–9

MESSAGE

I grew up in an extended family. My grandparents, aunt, and cousin lived with my mom, my sister, and me. It was a full house, always full of activity and never short of family drama with six females under one roof! In many respects, it felt like I had two mothers, and my cousin was like another sister. As unusual as it was, it worked for us and we were happy.

Sadly, death would come sooner and more often than we could have expected. Grandpa died when he was eighty-five years old; three years later my grandma died; and three months after that we lost our mom. It was a difficult period that reshaped the dynamics of our family forever. During a time of profound grief, Aunt Kellie cared for all three of us girls.

It wasn't until the roles reversed and I became the one to care for Aunt Kellie that I realized how difficult it must have been for her. Becoming a caregiver under difficult circumstances is something that Aunt Kellie and I now have in common. I love Aunt Kellie just as she loved us. Nevertheless, I often wonder if she ever felt some of the same resentments I now feel. Did she struggle with being forced to be the responsible adult, the one everyone relied on, the one to hold things together? Did she ever feel angry about being forced into a role she may not have chosen for herself?

The part of caregiving that no one wants to admit is the cycle of anger, hurt, resentment, and disbelief. I cringe when people tell me how well I treat my aunt. To be complimented on something that I feel resentful about fills me with guilt. These people wouldn't be so complimentary if they knew the thoughts that passed through my head. How I frequently dream of walking away and making someone else deal with the situation; how upset I am that my cousin and sister do not bear the same level of responsibility, how trapped I feel . . .

Aunt Kellie isn't the easiest person to get along with. She can be manipulative and enjoys pushing our buttons. She is extremely picky and makes comments that tear everything apart if something is not done to her satisfaction. She relies on others to make her happy and is negative unless others are there to please her. Aunt Kellie tests my patience in much the same way that we must have once tested hers, only I'm not always certain I pass the test.

I don't remember her being this way when we were younger. Something, somewhere became an anger that she couldn't escape. Was it grief? Was it responsibility? Was it loneliness? Or was she like me, wondering who would be left to take care of her? As a caregiver, when I am feeling down, I am usually grieving the loss of being cared for more than anything else. An unspoken truth among caregivers is that sometimes we simply miss being the child who was once cared for instead of being the one relied upon to provide care.

Kellie's daughter, my cousin Cindy, lives in another state. Their relationship is strained at best. Kellie is never invited to visit Cindy; she is not included for holidays and hardly knows her grandchildren. Cindy comes to visit for a day or two and acts like she can't wait to get out of town. Having lost both of my parents at young ages, I find it difficult to understand how anyone could be so far removed from her parent's life. It makes my heart ache for my aunt that her daughter doesn't want to spend time with her. Even though Aunt Kellie doesn't mention it, I know it has to hurt her. That, more than anything, makes me angry at my cousin.

Although at times I wish I didn't have to take so much responsibility for my aunt, I realize that my family and I are fortunate to have had the opportunity to have her in our lives—at my kids' graduations, birthdays, babies being born, holidays. As difficult as it had been, she is very important to us. She is so different from my own mother but definitely has been a substitute grandmother for my kids.

Aunt Kellie and I can drive each other crazy, but I know in her own way she loves me and deep down she appreciates what I do. She just has a hard time expressing it. I occasionally joke with her that it would be okay to let that love and appreciation bubble to the surface now and then.

Sometimes older people can get a little mean. I don't think age is an excuse to be hurtful. Aunt Kellie tries to play the "little old lady" card, but I call her bluff when she does. So many caregivers don't want to disagree with our elders "because they are old," but I don't believe it is disrespectful to expect good manners and kindness from them, just as we would from any family member.

Family caregiving can be messy, and it brings out the best and the worst in people. The reality is that not every responsibility is peacefully divided among family members. I've learned that family members can disagree and still love one another. I try not to get caught up in who should be doing what and stay focused on giving the best care that I am able to give. I am not alone. My wonderful family supports me, and God watches over me and refills my patience when I think I am at my wit's end.

Anonymous

"An unspoken truth among caregivers is that sometimes we simply miss being the child who was once cared for instead of being the one relied upon to provide care."

CAREGIVER'S PRAYER

Prince of Peace,

Thank you for supporting me during my caregiving trials. I don't know how I would make it through if you were not my source of strength. Help me to think upon those things that are positive and not dwell on the negative, frustrating aspects. Give me the energy and compassion I need to care for my loved one.

COSTLY DECISIONS

INTRODUCTION

I am definitely not the mathematician in our family—that would be my husband, Paul. He is always planning and charting goals. When we were first married, he kept a chart taped to the back of our closet that he would check periodically to see if we were financially on target. His main goal was to sell our first house within five years of its purchase. Would you believe it? Five years to the date, we sold that house! That is the power of writing down your goals. I am hoping some of his goal-setting ambition will rub off on me someday.

God tells us to be good stewards of our money. But that was not the case in this next story.

INSPIRATIONAL VERSE

Keep falsehood and lies far from me; give me
neither poverty nor riches, but give me only
my daily bread. Otherwise, I may have too
much and disown you and say, "Who is the
Lord?" Or I may become poor and steal, and
so dishonor the name of my God.

PROVERBS 30:8–9

MESSAGE

It's the bottom of the ninth inning; the bases are loaded,
my team is up by one run, and the opposing team's best
hitter is at the plate. He knows that a solid hit will win
the ball game. The look in his eye is unmistakable; he's
swinging for the fence. The coach points to me in the
bull pen and puts me in to save the game.

My hand is sweating inside my glove, and my heart
is pounding as I slowly walk to the pitcher's mound. I
keep looking to the dugout, wishing there were someone else to help, but there's no one else; I'm it.

I never find out who wins because it's always at this
moment that I wake up. When I wake I realize that the
batter standing at the plate is my dad, while the runner
on third base is my mom—and there are no other play-
ers on the field. The umpire's face is never revealed, but
the voice sounds similar to that of my wife. I don't know
exactly how to feel, but I do know it will take me a while
before I can shake the sense of it being me against them.

While in my dream it appears as if my parents are

about to win, in reality, a series of questionable financial decisions—or indecisions—has left them in a tough situation. Money is never an easy topic, and my parents refused to discuss their financial situation with us.

To make matters worse, when financial discussions were unavoidable, they refused any advice. Unfortunately, it's too late to reverse the damage, and their financial future is uncertain at best. I never have to see the end of my dream, because none of us wins if we can't work together.

Still, I wish I could help my parents. But it's difficult to help when they don't believe, or won't admit, they need help—meaning that my dream isn't far from the truth. I've always wished we could be on the same team, working toward a common goal. Unfortunately, they more often feel like rivals, dismissing my talents and resenting my efforts.

My wife and I both continue to offer solutions and options. We've learned that when we present information based on our professional expertise, my parents are more likely to respond positively. We have a functional relationship, and we're making incremental progress, but I certainly hoped for more.

If nothing else, however, my wife and I have learned from this situation, and we've put our own financial plans in place so that history won't repeat itself.

Illness and age have made my parents slowly face the repercussions of the decisions they've made along the way. We do care about them, but we're frustrated that it has come down to this. It's difficult to see them struggle unnecessarily.

They still refrain from being completely open about the extent of their situation, so I continue to live in fear of the 4:00 A.M. phone call that will require us finally to have that candid—and long overdue—discussion.

When that call comes, it really will feel like the bottom of the ninth with the bases loaded—the situation in which I do offer the team its last chance.

Anonymous

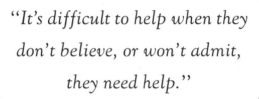

"*It's difficult to help when they don't believe, or won't admit, they need help.*"

CAREGIVER'S PRAYER

Dear Heavenly Owner of All,

You warn us that the love of money is the root of all evil. Help my spouse and me to manage our money wisely, and let us be content with our daily bread, which you graciously give to us. Help us to set financial goals for our future needs, and give us your Holy Spirit to guide us so we can follow through and make wise decisions.

MONEY CAN'T BUY

FORGIVENESS

INTRODUCTION

Forgive one another. Why is that so hard? Forgiveness reveals that we have made a mistake—we were wrong. Many people find that difficult to admit. Forgiveness also involves confessing. Confessing is being vulnerable, letting our guard down, opening ourselves up to possible attack and uncertainty about how our confession will be taken by another. This reminds me of Arthur Fonzarelli—the Fonz from *Happy Days*, who could never admit that he was "wrrrrong." Why is that so hard? Because of pride. Pride stands in the way of resolve. Many people will stay in their prideful misery for years instead of choosing to forgive and having that truly peaceful feeling.

Be quick to confess wrongdoing and be quick to forgive. It breaks my heart to hear of families such as Ann's who have been ripped apart because they could not forgive one another.

INSPIRATIONAL VERSE

Get rid of all bitterness, rage and anger, brawling and slander, along with every form of malice. Be kind and compassionate to one another, forgiving each other, just as in Christ God forgave you.

EPHESIANS 4:31–32

MESSAGE

My mother-in-law, Isabel, lived in a little house close to downtown, kept it neat, and had a garden to keep her busy. She was getting along nicely until one summer afternoon a young man broke the screen door and tied her to a chair. He cut the telephone line and robbed her. He had a knife, but he did not hurt her. Amazingly, he didn't find much money. Isabel pinched every penny ten times before she spent any, so money was there to be found: hidden under the floorboards, the table, and who knows where else. After the robber left, a neighbor eventually heard her yell and untied Isabel before I could get there. She was understandably upset and couldn't stay there anymore, so we brought her into our home.

We decided as a family that each of her three sons would keep Isabel for a few months at a time. Isabel stayed with my husband and me first, and then went to her oldest son's home. That lasted only two weeks before my sister-in-law said she couldn't do it anymore. Isabel had already decided she didn't want to go to her youngest son's house because he lived in the country and was never home. After a short stay with her sister, she ended back at our house.

We found a third-floor apartment that she liked, but as expected, the son who wouldn't keep her was critical of her choice. After Isabel's sister moved in across the hall following the death of her husband, the two were happy for many years.

Eventually Mom's mind started going. After realizing how expensive a nursing home would be, we asked if she'd like to live in our back room. This was the woman who would return half of an egg salad sandwich I made her for lunch because she had asked for only half, not a full sandwich. Isabel was of the generation that never wasted a penny, so you can imagine that spending three thousand dollars a month for nursing home care was more than she could comprehend. We charged her what she had been paying for rent, and she was delighted.

When she lost control of her bladder and bowels, we charged her more because of the additional work and expense in supplies, still a significant savings over the cost of a nursing home. The rest of the family seemed to ignore the savings or that she was being cared for by family and focused only on the fact that we were charging Isabel rent. Even though my husband and I were never after Isabel's money and were genuinely interested in giving her the best care, our motives were questioned by our family with every step we made. We never felt guilty for charging rent in exchange for caring for her at home as long as we were able.

The day arrived, however, when she needed more care than we could provide. Despite bitter words having been exchanged among them over the years, my husband invited his brothers to discuss a move to a nursing home. A heated argument ensued after his oldest brother said how awful it was that my husband had charged his own mom to live with us.

In some ways, I felt sorry that I had taken care of Mom, because none of the brothers had much to do with the others after that. Mom didn't live very long once she moved to the home, and my husband never visited her there. His brothers took a sudden interest and visited Isabel unusually often at the end. After her death, the eldest son and executor brought our share of the inheritance to the house, and that was the last time he was here. There was no thank-you for keeping her or for the money that we had saved her, just a check (larger than it would have been had she moved to the nursing home sooner) and a quick good-bye.

Before all this happened, the boys were close. If one was fixing something, one of the others would be helping. The family shared holidays, played cards on weekends, and enjoyed time together. It was sad to see the bond among brothers dissolve over money. Even more sad was that our pride stood in the way of Isabel being surrounded with love and peace among her sons as she passed away.

The man who forced Isabel from her home stole so much more than money. His actions that day cut deeper than any knife could have, and everyone in the family was robbed of the relationships they once knew. Isabel's sons did not speak again until we called them together at my dying husband's bedside four years later.

Forgiveness came at a price, much steeper than anyone should have to pay.

Ann Hess

"It was sad to see the bond among brothers dissolve over money. Even more sad was that our pride stood in the way of Isabel being surrounded with love and peace among her sons as she passed away."

CAREGIVER'S PRAYER

Forgiving God,

Help me to be understanding and open-minded when dealing with my family. Let me be quick to forgive those who wronged me and let me not hold grudges. I pray against arguments that separate us from our loved ones. Lord, help me to make peace with my family.

THE CHALLENGES OF
FAMILY CAREGIVING

INTRODUCTION

When I hear the word *sacrifice*, I immediately think of the ultimate sacrifice of our Lord and Savior Jesus Christ. My mind then turns to all of our men and women in the military services who lost their lives so that we could have our freedom. But is the sacrifice of a caregiver in an equivalent category? I believe it is. The soldier performs his duties out of love for his country; a caregiver performs hers out of love for her family. Both heroes put others before self.

Mark and his family are perfect examples of the sacrifices made on the home front in order to enhance and honor the life and health of a beloved parent.

MESSAGE

When Grandma Pearl (my husband's mother) came to live with us, everything changed. Life was harder and better at the same time. Life was different for all of us. Making room for Grammie proved to be a challenge for me; my husband, Mark; and our five children. Here are our stories.

Nancy I loved my mother-in-law and made the same promise to her as I did to my husband: "We'll take care of you." That's a big promise to make when we couldn't foresee the challenges it would bring.

Mark, my husband and the youngest of five, helped his mom, Pearl, care for his dad as cancer slowly took him away. As a result they share something deep and special. So when Pearl's Alzheimer's became too severe, she came to live with us, all eight of us in a small home.

Honestly, this tested me more than I could have imagined. There were moments when I second-guessed everything: who I was, what I believed in, why I was putting my children through this. Some nights it was all I could do to throw myself into bed and pray, "Please shape and mold me into the woman you want me to be and help me see the lessons you are giving to us." And sometimes I wasn't even sure what I was praying about. I just knew that our situation was in God's hands and that He would never fail me.

Caring for Pearl touched us as a family and individually in ways I could never have envisioned. We are all better for having shared her last years. Undeniably, our children became more compassionate and responsible. This life experience will make them better husbands, wives, mothers, fathers, and grandparents, but it came with a price. The reality is that making a promise and keeping it, when it affects your children, your sanity, and your marriage, are two very different things.

Please understand, I loved Pearl, but I struggled constantly with the guilt of asking my children to sacrifice. I struggled with resentment and feeling trapped. I felt like I was failing myself, my children, and my marriage. I couldn't be two places at once. I couldn't make more hours in the day. I couldn't be the wife, the mother, or even the Christian that I wanted to be.

But the resentments, grief, and guilt will eventually fade away, and what will remain is a family forever changed by the experience of caregiving. And just as we trusted God through it all, we have turned to Him now to help us heal and begin again.

Gabby I was eight years old when Grammie came to live with us. At first, I remember feeling mad. One day she was just my grandma tucking me in, the next she took my bed. Grammie also came with a lot of chores.

She needed so much help. And she took a lot of Mom's and Dad's time away from me.

On top of that, I was embarrassed to invite my friends to our house. I never knew what Grammie might do or say.

But I'll never forget this one day. We were all horsing around, and she was laughing just like us kids. That's when it struck me: If there was one person who I could always be myself around, no matter what, it was Grammie. After that, I would sit and talk to her about my days, even though she wouldn't remember it. She became the keeper of all my secrets. It may sound silly, but it was really special to me.

Ali G'ma, as I called her, started living with us when I was twelve. As the oldest child, I was expected to set the example, but all the while I kept asking "*Why?* Why wasn't I included in the decision?"

Living with G'ma wasn't easy—especially when she forgot her manners. She'd yell "*Coffee!*" instead of politely asking, "Can I have a cup of coffee please?" I got so tired of the same questions over and over again. Always the jokester, she'd hide our wallets in her laundry basket. She'd tell us she hated peanut butter, then eat it all. And every one of my boyfriends knew exactly how handsome she thought he was! Plus, we constantly worried about her safety and who was going to stay home with Grandma.

I don't want to sugarcoat it—all of this took its toll. Many times during her eight years with us, I became frustrated that it was as long a process as it ended up being.

Praying for it to end felt too much like asking God to take her from us, and that was a profound struggle for me.

We *probably* didn't do a lot of other things "*right*," but I wouldn't do anything different. By being with us, G'ma lived longer than she would have otherwise, and that alone made it worth it. She was part of our family, and for that we are grateful.

Bryce and Matt As the two youngest kids, we didn't understand why the rest of the family was so stressed about Grandma. Dad missed some of our games, but we understood that she needed him. Besides, we have him now. Grammie was our friend, and she was funnier than most comedians. She made animal noises and told jokes to make us laugh. Our family went through a lot just to take care of her, but we'll do the same thing for Mom and Dad someday. *Wouldn't everybody?*

Olivia In the beginning I didn't want Grammie to live with us. It was selfish, I know, but at age eleven I didn't want to share. With five kids, we already shared so much, including Mom and Dad.

Looking back, I can see how it brought us closer together though. With eight people living in the same house, we were always heading in different directions, but Grandma was the glue that held us together. Still, in some ways, she drove us apart.

In my heart I know the good outweighed the bad. But when you're in the moment of desperately needing more of your dad's attention and missing time with your mom, it isn't always so clear. We'd all do it again, but there has been damage in need of repair. My faith assures me that God will see us through, but in the meantime, we can't just pretend the pain away.

Someday the missed vacations and crammed house won't matter. What will matter is that we made Grammie's last years better. In fact, I learned great lessons about sympathy and compassion that could come only from this experience. Now when I see an older person who doesn't have what we gave Grammie, my heart breaks in an entirely different way.

Mark I fight back the tears as I listen to my family talk about having my mother live with us during her final years. Nothing they say necessarily surprises me, although it is still tough to hear. Did I fully appreciate the sacrifices that were made by my wife and kids as we cared for Mom? Did I listen to their struggles and frustrations? Had I considered the long-term effects having my mother live with us might have on my relationships with my own children?

The truth is I'm not really sure I thought about any of that at the time. It wasn't a topic open for discussion. I promised Mom that she would never step foot in a nursing home, and at any cost, I was keeping that promise.

So my family became a team of caregivers for Mom after her diabetes led to a stroke and eventually Alzheimer's. I worked days and spent my evenings with her while my wife and kids went to their sports, dances, activities. I missed out on a lot, but this was my mother, and in my mind, there was no other choice.

Even as her dementia worsened, Mom always knew me and became very demanding of my time. I didn't really mind. She often provided the perfect excuse to avoid family conflicts. She was consistent, and it was easy for me to care for her. As any man with three teenage daughters, two sons, and a wife balancing it all will tell you, it is easy to find comfort in consistency.

Mom and I had our evening ritual of building a fire and talking about our good times at the casino together. After her bathtime and bedtime, I was ready to be cared for myself. However, my needs were often met with resistance from a family who had already worked their shifts and simply needed more from me than I had left to give.

I knew our lives were being affected, but I believed our faith in God and family would prevail. Now, as I find my place again within my family, I realize the depth of that impact. Had I turned a blind eye to their needs so I could meet hers? Had I expressed my love to them enough through those years? Do they know how much it means to me that we were all there for my mother when she needed us?

I sacrificed being a fully attentive husband and father in order to be a good son. My lips tremble as I say the words out loud for the first time: "I put spending time with my mother over spending time with my own wife and kids, and that was more difficult than any of them could ever know."

Mark and Nancy Babe and Family

> "I promised Mom that she would never step foot in a nursing home, and at any cost, I was keeping that promise."

CAREGIVER'S PRAYER

God of Grace and Mercy,

I did not realize the price my family would have to pay for my decision to be a caregiver. Our family has endured many battle wounds and scars. Lord, I need your wisdom to make right choices today. Please increase my endurance, time, and energy just as you multiplied the bread and fish to minister to the crowd of five thousand. Your ultimate sacrifice resulted in victory; I know, with your mighty hand, I will be victorious too.

GOD'S GLORY

INTRODUCTION

Going to the beauty salon is so uplifting, especially when you are in dire need of hair color and highlights. I love going to my hairdresser, Linda, because she and I talk nonstop about what the Lord is doing in our lives and the lessons we have learned from our Bible studies. Linda's favorite prayer is "Lord, show me your glory," which she claims He does over and over. I decided, after leaving her salon, I would ask the Lord to show me His glory. Right then, the Lord said, "Look over your left shoulder." As I turned my head to the west, I saw the most spectacular Nebraska sunset I had ever seen. My mouth fell wide open—it was breathtaking! God said, "My glory is all around you, just look and see." As I looked around me, the orange and gold sunlight hit the blades of grass, and the leaves on the trees, illuminating the entire landscape. God made me realize that this glorious moment I was experiencing pales in comparison to the glory I will see someday in His presence.

Phyllis gives God the glory for inspiring her to care

for some special people who have made a significant impact on her life.

MESSAGE

I have spent my entire life, in one form or another, as a caregiver. As a granddaughter, mother, friend, and professional, I've had the honor to care for people who have changed my life. That's what caregiving does; it brings out the best in people. Caregiving bestows the single most important gift we can give to another human being: companionship. When that innate human need to feel connected and loved is met, people are stimulated, engaged, and feel good about themselves and the world around them. Caregiving, friendship, companionship, and connection all run along a two-way street, each reciprocating the others, and each making the others stronger.

My first caregiving experience was as a ten-year-old girl spending time with my grandparents. Of course, I didn't know I was a caregiver; I was just a granddaughter who loved her grandma and grandpa. My grandmother was blind as a result of high doses of cortisone used to treat her debilitating arthritis.

One of my favorite memories is taking walks uptown with Grandma. On her wheelchair hung a small basket of coins, which I could use to buy candy from the dime store for our walk home. I would describe the flowers or the trees that she could no longer see for herself. Though Grandma's vision had failed, she never neglected to see God's glory and taught me to see that He was everywhere. I secretly worried about how I would get her up the ramp when we got back home. But somehow, I always found the strength and knew she was right: He is everywhere.

My grandfather was a stroke victim, so my grandparents had a live-in "housekeeper"—before it was called caregiving—named Rose. In the evenings Rose would play the piano and my Dad would pick Grandma up from her wheelchair and dance with her. It wouldn't be until years later that I was able to appreciate everything my grandparents taught me, not through their words but through their actions. You wouldn't have known that either of them had physical limitations because their lives were full of love, and none of us saw either of them as limited.

I believe that when people feel loved and cared for, they don't dwell on the extent of their limitations as they do when they are lonely. Loneliness needs no help from age or illness; it takes the life right out of us on its own. A life void of friendship and full of loneliness can destroy the human spirit. Caregivers provide companionship that helps people rise above the situation they are in and live happier, more enriching lives.

A mother of one of my daughter's friends needed

someone to stay with her once a week while her care-giver was away. Like my grandfather, she was a stroke victim, and her communication skills were very limited. When I first arrived, she patted a spot on the couch for me to sit next to her, and we found an instant connec-tion. We started out as strangers and ended up as friends. Each week I spent with her, I left wiser and knowing more about myself, simply by having offered my time.

I am in my element working as an advocate for the elderly, and every single day I see God's glory at work. Giving my time and friendship to lift the spirits of oth-ers has been my best teacher and greatest reward.

I can't claim to have seen it all or to know any more than anyone else, but this I know for sure: When you remove the roadblocks and empower people to make a difference in the lives of others, people respond in ex-traordinary ways. The desire to improve the lives of oth-ers is woven into the DNA of caregivers, and it's magical when people are aligned to what's in their hearts.

Phyllis Hegstrom

"When you remove the roadblocks and empower people to make a difference in the lives of others, people respond in extraordinary ways."

CAREGIVER'S PRAYER

Glorious Creator,

Heaven and earth are filled with your glory. You have entrusted me to lift the spirits of some extraordinary individuals. Encourage my heart and strengthen me in every good deed and word as I advocate for seniors. Thank you for the many blessings that come from their friendship and companionship. Show me your glory, Lord, that I may praise you for your goodness.

SAVE A SPOT FOR ME

INTRODUCTION

As children growing up, we saved a place in the lunch line for our best friend, saved a seat next to us on the bus or at the movie theater for our boyfriend or girlfriend, and saved a special spot on our pillow for our beloved cat or dog.

Matthew West has a touching song called "Save a Place for Me." His lyrics talk about being thankful for the time he had with his loved one here and how he is dreaming of the day when he will finally be in heaven.

It is comforting to know that the Lord has a special place just for us in His Kingdom, where there is no more pain, no more sorrow, and no more separation. We have a special home together with Him in Eternity. Jeanne finds great comfort in this truth.

INSPIRATIONAL VERSE

"In my Father's house are many rooms; if it were not so, I would have told you. I am going there to prepare a place for you."

JOHN 14:2

MESSAGE

The pews were full of the friends and family who had come to honor the life of my mother. As I walked to the front of the sanctuary, all I could think was, I can't do this. I never liked public speaking, so I'm not sure what I was thinking when I decided to deliver the eulogy. It had been a long journey, and it was important for me to set my fears aside and honor my mother in death as beautifully as she had lived.

I focused for a moment on my dad and the empty spot next to him. Shaking, I took a deep breath and spoke from my heart. Mom was with me, as she had always been when I didn't believe I could do something, and somehow I managed to make it through.

We'd all made it through a lot of difficult moments in the last year and particularly in the final weeks before her death. After a long bout with cancer, she spent the last few days in a hospice center. She was at peace, and although physically weak, she was spiritually strong. Mom filled the room with her love and somehow managed to keep her family and friends laughing, even during her last moments awake.

She quietly slipped into a coma two days before she

died. She was smiling one minute and sleeping peacefully the next. My dad didn't leave her side other than to step into the hall when the nurses came to care for her. During one of those times, the nurses suggested, because of her breathing pattern, that it was time to bring in her family.

Telling the family that it was time to say good-bye to Mom was the hardest thing I have ever had to do. Saying those words out loud made it real to me. We'd become closer than ever during her illness, and although I didn't want her to suffer, I was also going to miss taking care of her.

The entire family gathered by her side and prayed. My dad, usually very stoic and not one to show emotion, kissed her lips and whispered something to her before leaving the room.

I realized then that there was someone else who would now need my care. I told Mom that it was okay and that I would take care of Daddy. It was at that very moment that she lifted her cheek and died. I went to the room where Dad was sitting by himself. I told him Mom had died and was now at peace.

Dad continued to live with us until the day he knew he needed full-time care. He was never one to ask for help, so it was a big deal to me that he asked to move into a care facility. He didn't want to be a burden. Although I never thought of him that way, I respected his decision and continued to visit him as often as I could.

When Dad passed away three years later, I was comforted by the words he had said to Mom during her final moments. As I kissed my father good-bye for the last time, I whispered to him, just as he had whispered to Mom, "Save a spot for me."

Jeanne Griffith

> *"We'd become closer than ever during her illness, and although I didn't want her to suffer, I was also going to miss taking care of her."*

CAREGIVER'S PRAYER

Sweet Promise Keeper,

Wrap your loving arms around those who are mourning the loss of a loved one. Give them strength and encouragement for the difficult days ahead and peace and comfort to heal their aching hearts. It is reassuring to know that you have personally prepared a place for our loved ones to dwell and to know that we will be reunited with them by way of your eternal plan and provision. Save a spot for me, Lord Jesus.

Caregiving Crusade

There is an army that quietly serves among us.
Its members are not camouflaged, and yet
They often go unnoticed, not seeking recognition or reward.

Some are recruited, others drafted, but more often than not,
These soldiers willingly join the ranks
Of those who give care when care is needed.
Theirs is not a war of despair or bloodshed
But rather a mission to protect our elderly, ill, and disabled.

Equipped with nothing more than love, compassion, and
    kindness,
These troops guard the dignity of aging parents,
Give comfort at the bedsides of dying friends and strang-
    ers alike,
Offer companionship to the lonely and hope to those who
    feel hopeless.

And deep within each of these honored souls is an eternal
    source of strength

That endures and fortifies caregivers.
The days are long, the challenges unyielding, the burdens
    heavy,
The victories small, the joys endless . . .
And yet they know that regardless of the situation
God abundantly and unconditionally provides
strength for the moment.

Melissa Collier
7-17-2011

Afterword

Thank you for reading *Strength for the Moment*. My hope is that it affirmed and encouraged you in some special way.

These stories have touched me too. I have gained insight into what caregiving really means. I have had a glimpse into the lives of caregivers and have come to a new level of respect and understanding for the compassion and devotion they bring to others in need. I have been moved by the joy and unexpected rewards that can come from any caregiving situation. Most of all, it is clear how faith in God sustains us through times of trouble. He is our ever-present help in time of need.

Did these stories touch your heart? I am interested in learning what lessons God taught you. I would be honored if you would share your thoughts or caregiving stories with me at *www.strengthforthemoment.com*.

Do you know someone who is a caregiver? If so, please share this book with them. It just may be the encouragement they need.

As you continue your caregiving journey, "May

the Lord bless you and keep you; the Lord make his face shine upon you and be gracious to you; the Lord turn his face toward you and give you peace" (Numbers 6:24–26).

....

If you would like additional information about caregiving, please visit www.caregiverstress.com. This website offers information and resources to help caregivers care for themselves while caring for others.

Contributors

Melissa and I enjoyed conducting interviews together with many of our contributors and going over other stories that were submitted to us in writing. As the family caregivers retold their personal stories, we were deeply touched by their heartfelt struggles and their times of joy.

Family

Catherine Hogan
Paul Hogan's mother, Omaha, NE
He Will Not Fail Me

Jan Novicki
Lori Hogan's mother, Omaha, NE
Easy Giving

Wendy Kuhn
Lori Hogan's sister, Omaha, NE
April Fools' Day!

Friends

Ann Hess
Retired mother of four sons, Artist & Craft Work,
    Jamestown, ND
Money Can't Buy Forgiveness

Bob Darrah
CPA, Council Bluffs, IA
Dentures and Dignity

Julie Hillmer
Bible Study Fellowship, Omaha, NE
All That Glitters Is Not Gold

LuAnn Anglo
Toastmaster, Life Coach, Caregiver, Papillion, NE
The Ladder of Love

Nancy and Mark Babe and Family
Omaha, NE
The Challenges of Family Caregiving

Rae Fischetti
Former College Administrator caregiving family,
The Last of the Golden Girls

Sarah Nordlund
Bible Study Fellowship, Omaha, NE
"Fore!"
Potter's Wheelchair

Tami Hillyer
Mosaic
My Highest Privilege

Business Associates
Georgene Lahm
President, GML Communications, Inc., Omaha, NE
No Hope?

Joe Pisani
Principal, The Dilenschneider Group, and
    Newspaper Columnist, New York
My Wife Is a Saint

Joe Tessitore
Publishing Consultant, New York
A Lover of Love . . . and of Jell-O

Melissa Collier
Freelance Writer, Moxie, Mo, Inc., Omaha, NE
Laughter Is a Precious Gift
The Boiling Pot
Caregiving Crusade

Home Instead Senior Care Franchise Owners
Becky Beanblossom
Louisville, KY
That's Just Peachy

Brad Snively
Frederick, MD
Living in Gratitude

Colette Hofelich
Louisville, KY, and New Albany, IN
Blissfully Unaware

Dana Goodman
Somerset, NJ
Brotherly Peace

Franny Fox
Marlton, NJ
Do It Now

Gary Leiter
North Kingston, RI
Wishes Come True

Geneva Labate
Riverside, CA
Rays of Light

James Gardenhire
Chattanooga, TN
When Dreams Fade

Laura Purcell
Melbourne, FL
God's Dominoes

Les Farnum
Charlotte, NC, and Huntersville, NC
The Hands of Time

Lucy Novelly
Pittsburgh, PA
A Daughter's Heart

Marge Thompson
Melbourne, FL
God's Dominoes

Marian Battersby
Grosse Pointe Woods, MI
Depths of Depression

Martin Warner
Toowong, Queensland, Australia
Heart and Soul

May Park
Seoul, South Korea
Turning Point

Sarah Warner
Toowong, Queensland, Australia
My Next Visit

Steve Nooyen
Green Bay, WI
Finding God's Lesson

Tracy Baugh
Lubbock, TX
Defying All Odds

Home Instead Senior Care Employees, Omaha, NE

Dan Wieberg
Public Relations Manager
Butterfingers
Lifelong Friend

Danielle Van Norman
Vendor Relationships Specialist
The Caring Doesn't End

Erin Albers
Marketing and Public Relations Manager
Just Breathe . . .

Jean Lynn
Human Resources Director
The Hand We're Dealt

Jeanne Griffith
Marketing Coordinator
Save a Spot for Me
Shower Me with Love

Jim Beck
Public Affairs Director
God Is Good and Does Right

Kay Shields
Training Coordinator
A Family Responsibility

Mary Alexander
Strategic Alliances Director
Selfless Service

Megan Mueller
Marketing Coordinator
Baby Sent from God

Phyllis Hegstrom
Advocacy Director
God's Glory

Rob Shradar
Vice President, Technology
Love Story

Tim Connelly
North American Franchise Development Director
Changing Perspectives

Yoshino Nakajima
Chief Development Officer
Two Countries, Two Homes

We wish to also acknowledge the contributors who chose to remain unnamed. While the bylines to these stories read "anonymous," these contributors offered candid and courageous insight. For this we are deeply grateful.

I Have My Own Life
Costly Decisions
Unspoken Truth

ABOUT THE AUTHOR

LORI HOGAN cofounded Home Instead Senior Care in 1994 with her husband, Paul. Now the largest nonmedical senior care company in the world, the Home Instead network has more than nine hundred independently owned and operated franchises in the United States and sixteen other countries. Lori plays a pivotal role in the growth of Home Instead by nurturing the culture of the company and enhancing relationships throughout the network.

Home Instead's Core Values
Honor God in all we do
Treat each other with dignity and respect
Encourage growth in ourselves and others
Build value in our service to others

Lori is a former Miss Nebraska USA and professional model, and she holds a psychology degree from the University of Nebraska at Omaha. She is involved in many philanthropic organizations in her community.

Bible Study Fellowship, in both the teaching and personal relationships, has been especially influential in Lori's spiritual journey.

In 2009, Lori and Paul coauthored the *USA Today* bestseller *Stages of Senior Care: Your Step-by-Step Guide to Making the Best Decisions*. The book serves as a comprehensive guide for understanding the ever-expanding world of senior care options.

To demonstrate their commitment to enhancing the lives of seniors everywhere, the Hogans became anchor donors for the Home Instead Center for Successful Aging. This unique partnership between the University of Nebraska Medical Center and Home Instead Senior Care is focused on a common goal: to find solutions with the potential to touch the lives of thousands or even millions of seniors around the world, and help seniors age more successfully.

Lori and Paul Hogan are proud to be the parents of Lakelyn, Mickele, Martin, and Jacquelyn. They reside in Omaha, Nebraska.

Profits from Strength for the Moment
that would accrue to the author will be donated to the
Home Instead Senior Care Foundation.

If you would like to learn more about the
Home Instead Senior Care Foundation,
we invite you to visit homeinsteadfoundation.com.